Silent Scars

Recovery and Freedom After Workplace Bullying and Gaslighting – Reclaiming Your Confidence, Voice, and Emotional Safety

Nicci Brochard
&
Dr. Ben Chuba

Silent Scars

Recovery and Freedom After Workplace Bullying and Gaslighting – Reclaiming Your Confidence, Voice, and Emotional Safety

CROSSBORDER
PUBLISHERS LLC

New York, London, Quebec

Contents

Introduction

In the modern workplace, most of us enter with hopes of building our careers, contributing meaningfully, and growing professionally. However, for too many, the work environment becomes a place of psychological torment—marked not by productivity and collaboration but by toxicity, manipulation, and emotional harm. Workplace bullying and gaslighting are two pervasive yet often overlooked forms of abuse that thrive in silence. They can rob an individual of their self-worth, erode their confidence, and leave emotional scars that are not always visible to the outside world.

Workplace bullying and gaslighting can occur in various forms: from overt harassment and intimidation to subtle tactics designed to undermine an individual's sense of reality and self-esteem. Unlike physical abuse, the wounds inflicted by workplace bullying are often invisible, leaving victims struggling in isolation, questioning their abilities, and doubting their worth. Gaslighting, the insidious manipulation where an individual is made to question their perceptions, memories, or sanity, often accompanies bullying, making the emotional damage even more profound. Victims of workplace bullying and gaslighting are often left feeling powerless, voiceless, and unsure of how to reclaim their personal and professional lives.

This book, *Silent Scars: Recovery and Freedom After Workplace Bullying and Gaslighting*, is an invitation to all those who have experienced the psychological toll of these toxic behaviors. It is a guide to recovery, self-empowerment, and emotional safety. It aims to provide survivors of workplace bullying with the tools and insights they need to heal from the scars left behind and reclaim their confidence, voice, and personal power. Whether you are currently suffering in silence or have already begun the healing journey, this book is designed to help you understand the dynamics of bullying and gaslighting, how to recognize these behaviors, and, most importantly, how to overcome their effects.

One of the central tenets of this book is that healing from workplace bullying and gaslighting is not only possible but necessary. The emotional scars left by these experiences can often lead to a loss of self-confidence, diminished self-worth, and a constant state of anxiety. Victims may feel trapped in their situation, uncertain of how to address the problem or whether their experiences are valid. The gaslighting tactics employed by abusers often lead to a sense of self-doubt and confusion, leaving victims unsure of what is real and what is manipulation.

Recovery, however, is possible. Reclaiming your emotional safety and confidence begins by recognizing that your experiences are valid and that you deserve to work in an environment that fosters respect and collaboration—not fear and manipulation. The first step in your recovery is understanding the patterns of workplace bullying and gaslighting, so you can begin to untangle the emotional damage and start the healing process.

As we embark on this journey through the chapters of this book, you will learn how to recognize the signs of bullying and gaslighting, both overt and subtle. You will gain insights into how these behaviors affect your emotional health and self-esteem. More importantly, you will discover practical tools to regain your confidence, establish your voice, and create emotional safety in your life. Whether you choose to remain in your current workplace or decide that it is time to move on, this book will help you navigate the emotional aftermath and take the steps necessary for rebuilding your life and career.

By the end of this book, you will have a deeper understanding of workplace bullying and gaslighting, and you will be empowered with strategies for emotional recovery. Most importantly, you will know that you are not alone. Healing takes time, but with the right tools and support, you can reclaim your confidence, rebuild your sense of self-worth, and find freedom from the scars left by toxic work environments. You have the right to work in a space where you are valued, respected, and emotionally safe, and this book will guide you toward that freedom.

Chapter 1

The Invisible Wound – Understanding Workplace Bullying and Gaslighting

Introduction:

When we think about workplace abuse, our minds often immediately conjure up images of overt aggression: yelling, slamming doors, or perhaps even physical confrontation. However, the reality of workplace bullying and gaslighting is often far more insidious and difficult to detect. These forms of psychological manipulation do not announce themselves with loud, dramatic outbursts; instead, they lurk beneath the surface, creeping into everyday interactions and slowly eroding an individual's sense of self. The invisible wound of workplace bullying and gaslighting is one that may not show up on medical charts or HR reports, but its effects are deeply felt, leaving lasting scars that can impact mental health, career performance, and personal relationships.

In this chapter, we will explore what workplace bullying and gaslighting really look like, uncovering the subtle, often hidden behaviors that characterize these toxic dynamics. We'll redefine the term "gaslighting" and explain how this form of psychological manipulation is used to distort reality and create confusion. Additionally, we'll examine why it's so difficult to name these behaviors in real time, often leaving victims feeling isolated and unsure of what's happening. We'll also delve into the common behaviors associated with workplace bullying and gaslighting, such as isolation, undermining, passive-aggression, and public shaming, that can slowly but surely break down the emotional and psychological well-being of the victim.

By the end of this chapter, you will have a clearer understanding of what constitutes workplace bullying and gaslighting and why they are so damaging. You will be better equipped to recognize the warning signs, understand the emotional toll they take, and begin the process of recovery.

What Workplace Bullying Really Looks Like (Not Just Yelling and Slamming Doors)

The first thing that often comes to mind when we hear the term "workplace bullying" is the image of a manager or colleague screaming, throwing things, or otherwise behaving in an overtly aggressive manner. This image, however, is only the tip of the iceberg. While physical aggression and yelling are certainly forms of workplace abuse, they do not represent the full spectrum of bullying behaviors that occur in many modern workplaces. Workplace bullying is much more subtle, often camouflaged as "tough leadership" or "feedback." It is the undercurrent of everyday interactions that leaves victims feeling worn down, anxious, and powerless.

Workplace bullying typically manifests in the following ways:

1. **Verbal Abuse (Not Just Yelling)**: While outright yelling can be a form of bullying, verbal abuse in the workplace takes many

forms. This includes belittling comments, sarcasm, hostile humor, or demeaning remarks disguised as "constructive criticism." These comments often leave the recipient feeling humiliated, confused, or angry but unsure how to respond without seeming overly sensitive or weak.

2. **Exclusion**: Bullying is often about power dynamics, and one of the most subtle and harmful forms of bullying involves isolating the target from social and professional networks. A colleague might subtly exclude you from meetings, exclude you from group emails, or fail to acknowledge your contributions. This exclusion creates feelings of loneliness, inadequacy, and self-doubt.

3. **Undermining Your Work**: A common bullying tactic is to deliberately undermine or sabotage someone's work. This could take the form of withholding important information, setting unrealistic expectations, or taking credit for your ideas. The goal is to diminish your confidence, sow seeds of self-doubt, and make you question your competence.

4. **Micromanaging**: This form of bullying typically involves a superior controlling every aspect of a subordinate's work, without room for autonomy or creativity. It sends the message that the person cannot be trusted to do their job, eroding their confidence and autonomy in the process.

5. **Threats and Intimidation**: Subtle threats, such as "You'd better be careful" or "That may not be good for your career," can be a form of bullying. These behaviors imply that there will be

negative consequences if the victim speaks out, undercuts their confidence, and traps them in a cycle of fear.

6. **Workload Overload**: Another insidious form of bullying involves placing impossible expectations on a person's workload—setting them up to fail by assigning more tasks than can reasonably be accomplished in a given timeframe. This leaves the person feeling overwhelmed, burned out, and helpless.

7. **Public Humiliation**: In some cases, workplace bullying involves embarrassing or shaming the victim in front of others. This might take the form of a manager or colleague criticizing someone's work publicly, ridiculing them in front of a group, or making their mistakes the subject of jokes. The goal is to diminish the target's credibility, making them feel smaller and less capable.

Workplace bullying is often subtle, persistent, and intended to make the victim feel isolated, incapable, and powerless. It is an ongoing pattern of behavior that wears down the victim over time, leaving them questioning their abilities and self-worth.

Gaslighting: Redefining Your Reality One Denial at a Time

Gaslighting is one of the most toxic and psychologically damaging forms of manipulation in the workplace. At its core, gaslighting is a tactic used by the abuser to make the victim doubt their perception of reality. The term originates from a 1944 film, *Gaslight*, in which a husband manipulates his wife into believing she is losing her sanity by subtly altering her environment and denying her experiences. In the workplace, gaslighting manifests as a pattern of psychological manipulation intended to confuse and destabilize the victim, making them question their memory, judgment, or even their sanity.

Gaslighting in the workplace can look like:

1. **Denying or Distorting Facts**: The gaslighter denies things they've said or done, even when there is evidence to the contrary. They might tell you, "I never said that," or "That never happened," leaving you confused and second-guessing your memory.

2. **Shifting Blame**: A gaslighter will frequently shift blame onto the victim, making them feel responsible for situations or mistakes that are not their fault. This tactic often involves minimizing the victim's feelings or concerns, while amplifying their own complaints.

3. **Making You Feel Overly Sensitive**: Gaslighters will often accuse the victim of being overly sensitive or "too emotional" whenever they try to express their discomfort. This tactic makes the victim question whether their emotional responses are justified or appropriate.

4. **Undermining Confidence**: Gaslighters will often make passive-aggressive remarks or provide contradictory feedback, leaving the victim uncertain of their abilities. Over time, this erodes their self-esteem and makes them more dependent on the gaslighter's version of reality.

5. **Manipulating Others Against You**: Gaslighters may also try to manipulate colleagues or superiors into believing negative things about the victim, painting them as unreliable, unstable, or difficult to work with. This is often done behind the scenes, leaving the victim unaware of the damage being done to their reputation.

Gaslighting makes it difficult for the victim to trust their own perceptions, leading to confusion, self-doubt, and ultimately, a breakdown in their sense of self. It is one of the most insidious forms of psychological abuse, as it often goes unnoticed by others and is hard to confront directly.

Why It's So Hard to Name What's Happening When It's Happening

One of the most perplexing aspects of workplace bullying and gaslighting is how difficult it is for victims to recognize what's happening to them while it's happening. Bullying and gaslighting don't always present as overt, violent behavior. In fact, many victims spend a significant amount of time doubting themselves, wondering if they are overreacting or being too sensitive. The abusers, on the other hand, are often skilled at rationalizing their behavior or making their actions seem benign.

Several factors contribute to this difficulty in recognizing workplace bullying and gaslighting:

1. **Normalization of Toxic Behavior**: In many toxic workplaces, bullying becomes so ingrained in the culture that it is normalized. A victim may feel that this is simply how work is supposed to be—stressful, competitive, and uncomfortable. The lines between acceptable behavior and abuse become blurred.

2. **Fear of Retaliation**: Victims may hesitate to name what's happening because they fear retaliation or being labeled as difficult, weak, or overly sensitive. Gaslighters, in particular, use this fear to keep their victims quiet, knowing that questioning the behavior could lead to further manipulation or even job loss.

3. **Self-Doubt and Internalized Blame**: Gaslighting makes victims question their perceptions, making it harder for them to pinpoint the abuse. Over time, they may internalize the blame, believing that they are the problem rather than acknowledging that the bullying or gaslighting is taking place.

4. **Lack of Awareness**: In many cases, victims of workplace bullying and gaslighting are unaware of the emotional and psychological toll these behaviors are taking. They may not recognize the long-term effects of constant undermining, isolation, or manipulation, making it difficult to identify the abuse as it occurs.

5. **Manipulative Appearances**: Bullies and gaslighters are often very skilled at presenting themselves as reasonable, caring, or authoritative figures. They can easily convince others that they are simply "tough" or "demanding," which leaves victims

questioning whether they're overreacting or misinterpreting the situation.

The difficulty in naming the abuse while it's happening is one of the most insidious parts of the experience. It creates a sense of isolation, confusion, and powerlessness that leaves victims trapped in a cycle of self-doubt and emotional pain.

Common Behaviors: Isolation, Undermining, Passive-Aggression, and Public Shaming

Several common behaviors are indicative of workplace bullying and gaslighting. Understanding these behaviors can help you recognize the signs of abuse and begin to reclaim your emotional and psychological well-being.

Isolation

Isolation is one of the most common tactics used by workplace bullies. By distancing the victim from others—either through exclusion from meetings, withholding information, or creating a hostile work environment—they weaken the victim's sense of community and support. Isolation leaves the victim feeling alone and unsupported, making them more vulnerable to the manipulative tactics of the abuser.

Undermining

Undermining is another key feature of workplace bullying. It involves sabotaging or diminishing the victim's contributions, skills, or work. Bullies may take credit for the victim's ideas, give them unrealistic workloads, or actively create obstacles that prevent them from succeeding. This behavior is designed to make the victim feel unworthy, incompetent, and powerless.

Passive-Aggression

Passive-aggressive behaviors are subtle yet incredibly damaging. Bullies may employ indirect tactics such as sarcasm, backhanded compliments, or intentional neglect. These behaviors are difficult to pinpoint, as they don't involve direct confrontation. However, over time, they create an environment where the victim feels constantly undermined and unsure of how to respond.

Public Shaming

Public shaming is one of the most humiliating forms of workplace bullying. It can involve reprimanding the victim in front of others, mocking them, or exposing their mistakes to a group. Public shaming is meant to strip the victim of their dignity and establish the bully's dominance. It often leaves the victim feeling humiliated, isolated, and devalued.

Conclusion

Workplace bullying and gaslighting may not be as immediately obvious as other forms of workplace abuse, but their effects can be just as damaging, if not more so. The invisible wounds they create are often the hardest to heal because they involve subtle, ongoing manipulation and emotional manipulation that leaves the victim questioning their reality and self-worth. Recognizing these behaviors is the first step in reclaiming your emotional safety and healing from the trauma they cause.

Chapter 2

You're Not Too Sensitive – Validating the Emotional Impact

Introduction

In many workplaces, there exists a pervasive myth that employees who are sensitive to mistreatment, bullying, or emotional manipulation are simply "too thin-skinned" or overly dramatic. This myth is often used to gaslight individuals, making them feel as if their emotional responses to toxic work environments are invalid or unreasonable. The reality, however, is that workplace bullying and toxic behavior can have profound emotional and psychological effects on employees—effects that are often dismissed, downplayed, or ignored altogether.

This chapter aims to validate the emotional impact of workplace bullying and gaslighting, recognizing that these experiences are not just "toughened up" or "brushed off" as workplace realities. Instead, bullying has a real, lasting effect on an individual's mental health and self-worth. It distorts their perception of themselves and leads to trauma responses that can extend far beyond the office. By understanding the ways in which bullying corrodes self-worth, causes mental health damage, and leads to trauma responses like over-apologizing, self-doubt, and hypervigilance, we can begin to dismantle the harmful myth of the "thin-skinned" employee. More importantly, we can acknowledge and affirm the real emotional toll that workplace abuse takes, and the need for genuine healing and recovery.

The Myth of the "Thin-Skinned" Employee

The term "thin-skinned" is often wielded as a weapon in toxic workplaces, used to dismiss employees who react emotionally to mistreatment or manipulation. Employees who show visible signs of distress when bullied may be labeled as "overly sensitive" or unable to handle stress, when, in fact, their emotional reactions are entirely valid and warranted. This myth implies that if you are affected by mistreatment, the problem lies with you, rather than with the behavior of your abuser.

This narrative is particularly damaging because it shifts the blame onto the victim rather than confronting the real issue—the bully's behavior. The culture of "toughening up" in response to workplace bullying not only invalidates the victim's feelings but also reinforces the idea that emotional pain resulting from bullying is something to be ignored or suppressed. It encourages employees to endure harm in silence, perpetuating cycles of abuse and creating a toxic work environment.

In reality, it is perfectly natural to feel upset, frustrated, or hurt when subjected to bullying. Being called "thin-skinned" invalidates the emotional experience of the victim and discourages them from speaking out. It enforces silence and perpetuates the cycle of abuse, making it harder for the individual to seek help or validate their feelings. The emotional responses that victims exhibit are not signs of weakness or fragility—they are indicators of the harm being inflicted on their mental health and sense of self-worth.

By recognizing and validating these emotional responses, we can shift the focus from blaming the victim to addressing the root cause: the bully and the toxic work environment they've created.

How Bullying Corrodes Self-Worth and Mental Health

The psychological effects of workplace bullying extend far beyond the immediate feelings of hurt or frustration. Over time, the constant emotional abuse can deeply affect a person's self-worth and mental health, leaving lasting scars that may not be visible to others but can severely affect the individual's life and well-being.

Workplace bullying, especially when it is prolonged, can cause significant damage to an individual's self-esteem. Employees who are frequently belittled, isolated, or manipulated begin to internalize the criticism they receive. Over time, they come to believe that they are incapable, incompetent, or unworthy of respect. This self-doubt can take many forms:

- **Imposter Syndrome**: Victims of bullying often develop imposter syndrome—the belief that they are frauds, undeserving of their position, or that their accomplishments are due to luck rather than skill. This feeling can be exacerbated when the bully continuously undermines or belittles the individual's contributions.

- **Loss of Confidence**: The constant undermining of one's abilities or ideas can erode confidence. Victims may find themselves second-guessing their decisions, questioning their skills, and fearing judgment from others. This lack of confidence can lead to hesitancy in taking on new challenges, stifling growth and development.

- **Social Withdrawal**: As bullying isolates the victim from colleagues or their team, it can also cause them to withdraw socially. The victim may begin to avoid social events or shy away from work-related discussions, fearing further criticism or ridicule. This withdrawal can increase feelings of loneliness and further reduce self-worth.

The mental health consequences of workplace bullying are equally significant. Victims often experience anxiety, depression, and chronic stress. These conditions are not just reactions to stress but often evolve into more persistent mental health struggles when the abuse is ongoing or unaddressed. Bullying can disrupt an individual's ability to focus, concentrate, or perform at their best, leading to a decrease in productivity and even physical symptoms such as fatigue, headaches, or digestive issues.

In extreme cases, victims may experience burnout, a state of physical, emotional, and mental exhaustion caused by prolonged stress. Burnout can make individuals feel emotionally numb, detached from their work, and unable to recover from the exhaustion caused by constant abuse.

The long-term effects of bullying can also extend into other areas of life, affecting personal relationships and overall quality of life. A person who has been subjected to emotional abuse may find it difficult to maintain healthy relationships outside of work, often due to diminished trust, feelings of worthlessness, or the inability to set healthy boundaries.

Ultimately, bullying erodes a person's self-concept, making them feel inadequate, incapable, and unworthy of respect. Healing from this damage requires both recognizing and addressing the harm done to mental health and self-worth and reclaiming the confidence and emotional safety that was taken away.

Recognizing Trauma Responses: Over-Apologizing, Self-Doubt, Hypervigilance

Workplace bullying and gaslighting often lead to trauma responses, where the victim's body and mind react to stress and manipulation in ways that are shaped by the abuse they've endured. These responses, although natural reactions to prolonged mistreatment, can become ingrained patterns that are difficult to break. Understanding and recognizing these trauma responses is an important step in the recovery process.

Over-Apologizing

One common trauma response to workplace bullying is over-apologizing. Victims often begin to apologize excessively, even when they haven't done anything wrong. This is a learned behavior that emerges from constant criticism or blame from the abuser. When a person is constantly told that they are wrong, incompetent, or to blame for something, they start to apologize for almost every action or decision they make, even in situations where an apology is unnecessary.

Over-apologizing is a way of preemptively diffusing potential conflict or avoiding further criticism. It stems from a place of fear and insecurity—fear of being blamed or chastised again. This behavior often comes from a lack of confidence and the belief that everything they do is wrong or deserving of punishment. Over time, this pattern can chip away at an individual's sense of autonomy and self-worth.

Self-Doubt

Self-doubt is another key trauma response, especially in the wake of gaslighting and constant undermining. Victims of workplace bullying often begin to second-guess their abilities, decisions, and perceptions. They may have been told repeatedly that they're not good enough or that their experiences and feelings aren't valid, leading them to question their own judgment and self-worth.

This self-doubt can manifest in various ways, such as:

- **Constantly seeking validation from others**: The victim becomes overly dependent on feedback from others to determine their worth and competency.

- **Feeling incapable of making decisions**: Due to constant undermining, the victim may struggle with making decisions, even simple ones, because they no longer trust their judgment.

Self-doubt not only affects an individual's ability to perform at work but also affects their personal life. Victims of bullying may start doubting their ability to be good partners, friends, or family members, perpetuating a cycle of low self-esteem and emotional pain.

Hypervigilance

Hypervigilance is another trauma response commonly seen in individuals who have been subjected to bullying and gaslighting. It's a heightened state of awareness, where the victim is constantly scanning their environment for signs of danger, conflict, or criticism. This response is a survival mechanism that helps the victim anticipate harm before it occurs, but it can also lead to chronic stress and anxiety.

Hypervigilance can cause individuals to feel constantly on edge, unable to relax or let their guard down. This leads to fatigue, anxiety, and an inability to focus or concentrate, as the mind is always preoccupied with potential threats or negative interactions. In the workplace, this might manifest as avoiding certain people or situations, overthinking interactions, or becoming hyper-focused on pleasing others to avoid criticism or retribution.

Over time, hypervigilance can be emotionally and physically exhausting, preventing the victim from feeling safe or at ease, even when they are no longer in immediate danger.

Workplace PTSD is Real – and Common

While workplace bullying and gaslighting may seem like intangible problems, the emotional and psychological effects they have on victims are real and long-lasting. Post-Traumatic Stress Disorder (PTSD), typically associated with traumatic events like natural disasters or military combat, can also arise from prolonged exposure to workplace bullying and gaslighting.

Workplace PTSD is a form of trauma caused by chronic exposure to emotional abuse, manipulation, and toxic work environments. It results in a range of symptoms similar to those seen in survivors of other traumatic experiences, including:

- **Intrusive thoughts or flashbacks**: Victims may have constant, uncontrollable memories of bullying incidents that disrupt their daily lives.

- **Avoidance**: Victims may avoid certain places, situations, or even colleagues because they associate them with the trauma they experienced.

- **Emotional numbness**: Survivors may disconnect from their emotions or feel detached from their environment as a coping mechanism.

- **Difficulty trusting others**: Trust is often shattered after experiencing betrayal and manipulation, leading to difficulty in forming or maintaining relationships.

- **Hyperarousal**: Increased anxiety, irritability, and exaggerated startle responses are common signs of PTSD in the workplace.

Workplace PTSD is often minimized or ignored because it doesn't have the obvious, physical symptoms that other forms of trauma might display. However, it is just as real and damaging. Victims need

Chapter 3

The Anatomy of Power Abuse – Why Bullies Target Certain People

Introduction

Workplace bullying is rarely a random occurrence; it is a calculated tactic used by individuals who seek to exert control over others. While many may assume that bullies target the "weak" or those who are perceived as vulnerable, the reality is more complicated. Bullies often choose their targets based on specific personality traits that they perceive as threatening to their own sense of power, status, or control. Understanding why certain individuals are targeted, and why they fall victim to such manipulation, is crucial for breaking the cycle of abuse and finding a path to recovery.

In this chapter, we will delve into the anatomy of power abuse in the workplace, exploring the personality traits that bullies often target, the role of narcissistic leadership and insecure managers in fostering a culture of bullying, and why HR sometimes protects the problem rather than solving it. We will also examine the role of groupthink and silent bystanders in perpetuating workplace bullying. By understanding these dynamics, we can better recognize and resist the forces that allow workplace bullying to thrive.

The Personality Traits Bullies Often Pick On (Hint: It's Not Weakness, It's Strength)

The stereotype of the "weak" target of bullying is one that is frequently perpetuated by both the bully and the broader workplace environment. However, in reality, bullies often target individuals who possess certain personality traits that threaten their own sense of control or dominance. This is a key distinction to make: bullies are not looking for the weak or powerless; they are looking for those who have qualities that challenge their authority or make them feel insecure.

Some of the traits that make people more likely to be targeted by workplace bullies include:

Empathy and Compassion

Individuals who demonstrate empathy or compassion often make excellent leaders, team players, and colleagues. However, these traits can also make them targets for bullies. Empathetic individuals are more likely to be sensitive to others' needs and emotions, and their caring nature makes them appear vulnerable to exploitation. Bullies may view empathetic employees as easy targets for manipulation, using their kindness against them in a way that causes emotional harm.

Competence and High Standards

While bullies often target those they perceive as "weak," they also frequently go after employees who are competent, hardworking, and dedicated. High-performing individuals who consistently produce results or demonstrate exceptional skills may be seen as a threat to those in positions of power, especially when those in power feel insecure or inadequate. Rather than celebrating success, bullies may attempt to undermine these individuals, either through sabotage, criticism, or undermining their achievements, to diminish their perceived threat.

Independent Thinkers

Employees who ask tough questions, challenge the status quo, or offer creative solutions can become prime targets for bullies. These individuals are often seen as "troublemakers" by those who fear disruption or change. Bullies, particularly those with narcissistic tendencies, will often target people who are independent thinkers because they pose a direct challenge to the established hierarchy or group dynamic. Instead of encouraging growth and innovation, bullies will seek to suppress these employees' contributions by belittling or isolating them.

Strong Moral Compass

Individuals with a strong moral compass—those who consistently stand up for what is right, who challenge unethical behavior, or who advocate for fairness—often find themselves targeted by bullies who thrive in toxic or corrupt environments. A person's ability to challenge authority or stand up to injustice makes them a perceived threat to bullies who rely on power dynamics, manipulation, or unethical practices to maintain control. Bullies may attempt to discredit, isolate, or intimidate these individuals to prevent them from standing in the way of their agenda.

People-Pleasing and Desire to Help

Interestingly, those who are people-pleasers or individuals who consistently put others' needs before their own can also become targets. While this behavior often stems from a desire to avoid conflict or gain approval, bullies can exploit this tendency, pushing these individuals to do more than they should, taking advantage of their willingness to help. These targets may find themselves overloaded with work or put in positions where their boundaries are consistently crossed, causing emotional exhaustion.

The key point here is that bullying often arises from a deep sense of insecurity in the bully. They target individuals who, while not weak, possess traits that make them appear threatening or challenging to their authority. These traits are often misinterpreted by the bully as weaknesses because they are perceived as vulnerabilities to exploit. In reality, these traits reflect inner strength, empathy, and moral integrity—qualities that bullies, particularly those in positions of power, seek to diminish.

Narcissistic Leadership and Insecure Managers

The role of leadership in perpetuating workplace bullying cannot be overstated. Narcissistic leaders and insecure managers often create an environment that fosters bullying, either through direct action or through passive tolerance of toxic behavior. These individuals, consumed by their own need for control, validation, or dominance, view their subordinates not as valuable team members but as tools for personal gain or as obstacles to be removed.

Narcissistic Leadership

Narcissistic leaders are particularly dangerous in the context of workplace bullying. These leaders are driven by an inflated sense of self-importance, a deep need for admiration, and a lack of empathy for others. They are often blind to the emotional and psychological harm they cause, as their primary concern is maintaining their power and sense of superiority. Narcissistic leaders may bully others to reinforce their control, demand blind obedience, and make decisions that serve their interests rather than the collective good.

Common traits of narcissistic leadership include:

- **Lack of empathy**: Narcissistic leaders fail to consider the emotional impact of their actions on others, and they may belittle or dismiss the concerns of their subordinates.

- **Exploitation**: They may use people for personal gain, taking credit for others' work and making those around them feel undervalued.

- **Favoritism**: Narcissistic leaders may play favorites, creating division within teams and fostering an environment of insecurity and competition.

- **Blame-shifting**: When things go wrong, narcissistic leaders will often deflect blame onto others, making their employees feel responsible for failures.

Narcissistic leaders often create a toxic work environment where bullying becomes normalized, and victims of bullying may feel powerless to address the issue because their abuser is the one in charge. The toxic leadership style sets the tone for the entire organization, leaving those lower in the hierarchy to fend for themselves in an environment where bullying goes unchecked.

Insecure Managers

Insecure managers—those who feel threatened by the competence, achievements, or success of their subordinates—are also key contributors to the culture of workplace bullying. These managers may use bullying tactics to keep their employees in check, attempting to maintain control over them by asserting dominance or undermining their confidence. Instead of fostering an environment of collaboration, these insecure managers create an atmosphere of fear and hostility.

Insecure managers often feel the need to micromanage, critique employees excessively, or dismiss their contributions, all of which are forms of bullying. They may bully individuals who are more competent or capable, seeing them as a threat to their position or status. By keeping employees uncertain of their abilities or constantly questioning their worth, these managers attempt to safeguard their own insecurities, rather than building a cohesive and effective team.

Culture of Silence: Why HR Sometimes Protects the Problem

One of the most frustrating aspects of workplace bullying is the culture of silence that often surrounds it. Employees who experience bullying may be reluctant to speak out, fearing retaliation, being labeled as troublemakers, or simply not being believed. Worse, Human Resources (HR), the department charged with addressing employee grievances, may fail to take meaningful action or, in some cases, may actively protect the bully. This culture of silence perpetuates the toxic environment and makes it difficult for victims to escape the cycle of abuse.

Lack of Action from HR

In many workplaces, HR departments are not equipped or motivated to effectively address bullying. Often, HR's primary role is seen as protecting the company from liability rather than supporting employee well-being. As a result, HR may downplay complaints, dismiss allegations of bullying as personal disputes, or fail to properly investigate claims. In some cases, HR might even cover up the bullying behavior if the person responsible is in a position of power or influence.

HR's failure to act contributes to the culture of silence, where victims feel powerless and unsupported. When bullying is ignored or swept under the rug, it sends the message that such behavior is tolerated or even condoned, perpetuating the cycle of abuse.

Fear of Retaliation

Another reason why HR may protect the problem is the fear of retaliation. Employees who report bullying often face retaliation in the form of further harassment, demotion, or even termination. HR may feel compelled to protect the perpetrator, especially if they hold a senior position, to avoid escalating the situation. This creates a toxic work environment where the bully is allowed to continue their behavior unchecked, while the victim is left to suffer in silence.

The Role of Groupthink and Silent Bystanders

Workplace bullying does not happen in a vacuum. Often, it is enabled by a culture of groupthink, where employees either silently witness the abuse or, worse, participate in it. Silent bystanders play a key role in perpetuating the cycle of bullying, whether they are aware of it or not.

Groupthink

Groupthink occurs when the desire for harmony and conformity within a group leads to irrational or dysfunctional decision-making. In workplaces where bullying is prevalent, groupthink can manifest in the form of ignoring or downplaying toxic behaviors to avoid rocking the boat. Employees may be hesitant to speak out against a bully, particularly if they perceive the bully as powerful or if there is a culture of avoiding conflict at all costs.

Groupthink creates an environment where bullying becomes normalized, and dissenting voices are suppressed. When everyone within the group remains silent or passive in the face of abuse, it reinforces the power dynamics at play and makes it difficult for the victim to seek support.

Silent Bystanders

The role of silent bystanders is critical in perpetuating bullying. While they may not actively participate in the abuse, their failure to intervene or speak up allows the bully's behavior to continue unchecked. Some employees may fear becoming targets themselves, while others may simply be unaware of the harm being caused. Regardless of the reason, silent bystanders enable the bully to maintain power and control.

Conclusion

The anatomy of workplace power abuse is complex and deeply embedded in organizational culture. Bullies don't target the "weak"; they target those who pose a threat to their sense of control, such as empathetic individuals, competent workers, and independent thinkers. Narcissistic leadership and insecure managers exacerbate the problem by fostering environments where bullying becomes normalized, and HR departments often fail to act or protect the problem. Groupthink and silent bystanders further perpetuate the cycle of abuse, leaving victims feeling isolated and powerless.

Understanding the dynamics of power abuse is crucial for both identifying bullying behavior and creating a culture of accountability in the workplace. By recognizing the traits that make certain individuals targets and examining the role of leadership, HR, and bystanders, we can begin to dismantle the structures that allow bullying to thrive. Only then can we create workplaces where all employees are treated with dignity, respect, and fairness.

Chapter 4

The Turning Point – Recognizing the Moment It Changed You

Introduction

There comes a moment in the journey of workplace bullying and gaslighting when everything shifts. It's the turning point—the moment when you realize that you are not the problem, that the pain, confusion, and emotional turmoil you've been enduring are not a reflection of your weakness or inadequacies, but rather the result of toxic behavior and abuse. This moment, often referred to as the "snap" moment, can be jarring, freeing, and incredibly empowering. It is the moment you begin to see clearly, to step out of the fog of manipulation, and to reclaim control over your narrative.

In this chapter, we will explore the significance of that turning point—the moment when you realize that what has been happening to you is not your fault, and that you have the power to change the course of your recovery. We will discuss how to retell your own story, not with shame or distortion, but with the clarity and strength that comes from acknowledging the truth. We will also delve into the often unspoken grief that accompanies this realization: the loss of trust, identity, and passion. Recognizing and acknowledging this grief is an important part of healing, as it allows you to honor what has been lost and begin to rebuild your sense of self.

The "Snap" Moment: Realizing It's Not You, It's Them

For many survivors of workplace bullying and gaslighting, there is a pivotal moment when everything changes. It may be a specific event, a particular comment, or simply the culmination of ongoing mistreatment. Whatever it is, this moment offers clarity, like a light bulb turning on after a long period of confusion. It's the realization that the problem is not with you, but with the toxic behavior of those around you.

This moment is often described as the "snap" moment, when you suddenly understand that the mistreatment you've been enduring is not a reflection of your inadequacies or failures, but the result of someone else's manipulative behavior. It might come after months or years of doubt, confusion, and questioning. Perhaps you've spent countless hours replaying interactions in your mind, wondering if you're being overly sensitive or misinterpreting the situation. Or, perhaps, you've tried to address the issue, only to be met with denial, deflection, or blame-shifting.

But the snap moment is when it all becomes clear. You realize that you've been gaslit into questioning your reality. You recognize that your feelings and experiences are valid, and that it's not you who is flawed, but the toxic individuals who have been abusing their power. You understand that you've been trapped in a system of manipulation, and that the emotional pain you've been feeling is not a reflection of your shortcomings, but of the emotional abuse being inflicted upon you.

This realization can be both liberating and overwhelming. It may bring a sense of relief, as if a weight has been lifted, but it can also bring an intense flood of emotions—anger, frustration, grief, and disbelief. The snap moment is the beginning of a new phase in your journey, one where you start to reclaim your power, trust your own perceptions, and break free from the hold of those who have manipulated you.

Embracing the Truth: The Power of Clarity

Recognizing that the abuse was never about you is the first step toward healing. It's a truth that takes time to fully internalize, but it's a crucial one. For so long, you may have believed that your worth was tied to how well you could meet the expectations of others. You may have believed that your emotional responses were exaggerated or unwarranted. But once you realize that the mistreatment you've faced is not a reflection of your inadequacy, it becomes easier to let go of the guilt and shame that often accompany these experiences.

The clarity gained from this moment allows you to begin to set boundaries and regain control over your emotional safety. You can start to reject the toxic behaviors that have been normalized and begin to build a healthier relationship with yourself. The snap moment is the catalyst for change, marking the point where you stop blaming yourself and begin to reclaim your power.

Retelling Your Own Story Without Shame or Distortion

One of the most powerful ways to heal after workplace bullying and gaslighting is to retell your own story. However, this process is often complicated by the shame and distortion that has been imposed on you. Gaslighting, in particular, makes it difficult for victims to trust their own memories and perceptions. After repeated denial and manipulation, you may begin to doubt the reality of your experiences, or you may feel ashamed of your emotional reactions to the mistreatment you've endured.

But retelling your story without shame or distortion is essential for reclaiming your sense of self and beginning the healing process. This is the moment when you stop internalizing the gaslighter's version of events and start speaking your truth. Your experiences—your feelings, your perceptions, your pain—are valid, and you have the right to tell your story as it truly is.

Finding Your Voice

When you've been silenced or manipulated for a prolonged period, finding your voice again can be daunting. You may worry about being judged or dismissed. But speaking your truth—whether to yourself, to trusted friends or colleagues, or in a formal report—is a critical step in breaking free from the cycle of abuse. Your voice is powerful, and reclaiming it is an essential part of the healing process.

One way to begin retelling your story is by journaling. Writing down your experiences, your emotions, and your reflections can be a therapeutic exercise that allows you to express yourself freely and without judgment. It also provides a concrete record of your experiences, which can be helpful when navigating the process of recovery.

Another way to retell your story is by speaking it aloud to someone you trust. This could be a close friend, family member, or therapist. Verbalizing your experiences can help you process your emotions, gain validation, and gain perspective on the situation. Having someone listen to your story without judgment or interruption can be incredibly healing and reaffirming.

Retelling your story without shame or distortion is not about seeking validation or approval from others; it's about acknowledging your own truth and standing firm in it. It's a powerful act of reclaiming your self-worth and beginning the journey of healing.

Acknowledging the Silent Grief: Loss of Trust, Identity, Passion

One of the less visible but deeply impactful consequences of workplace bullying and gaslighting is the silent grief that accompanies the loss of trust, identity, and passion. These losses are not always immediately apparent but can have a profound effect on an individual's emotional and psychological well-being. Recognizing and grieving these losses is a critical part of the healing process.

Loss of Trust

Workplace bullying and gaslighting often lead to a fundamental loss of trust—both in others and in yourself. When you've been manipulated, lied to, or belittled for an extended period, it becomes difficult to trust anyone, including your colleagues, supervisors, or even yourself. The gaslighting and manipulation you've experienced distort your reality, leaving you uncertain of who to trust or what is real.

This loss of trust can extend beyond the workplace, affecting personal relationships and making it harder to form new, healthy connections. Healing requires the slow process of rebuilding trust—starting with yourself. Relearning to trust your own judgment and instincts is an essential part of regaining your emotional safety.

Loss of Identity

Workplace bullying and gaslighting can also lead to a profound loss of identity. Over time, constant criticism, undermining, and manipulation can cause you to doubt your abilities, your worth, and your sense of self. You may have spent so much time trying to please others or meet their expectations that you lose sight of who you are and what you stand for.

Reclaiming your identity involves rediscovering what you value, what you're passionate about, and what you believe in. It's about recognizing that your worth is not defined by how others treat you but by your inherent qualities and contributions. Rediscovering your identity is an empowering part of healing, as it allows you to rebuild a sense of self that is no longer tied to the toxic dynamics of your workplace.

Loss of Passion

Finally, the loss of passion is one of the quieter but more profound consequences of workplace bullying and gaslighting. When you've been subject to ongoing mistreatment, your enthusiasm for your work, your career goals, and even your life outside of work can diminish. Bullying can strip away the joy and passion you once had for your job, leaving you feeling burned out, uninspired, and emotionally exhausted.

Reclaiming your passion involves reconnecting with the reasons you pursued your career in the first place. It's about finding new sources of inspiration, setting new goals, and rediscovering what excites and motivates you. Healing from this loss is a slow process, but it is an essential part of moving forward and rebuilding a fulfilling life and career.

Conclusion

The turning point in the journey of recovery from workplace bullying and gaslighting is a powerful moment of clarity—the "snap" moment—when you realize that the mistreatment you've endured is not your fault, and that the toxic behaviors of others are what have caused the pain. This moment marks the beginning of reclaiming your voice and retelling your story without shame or distortion. It is a pivotal step in breaking free from the psychological manipulation that has kept you trapped in a cycle of self-doubt and emotional harm.

Acknowledging the silent grief of loss—trust, identity, and passion—is also a crucial part of the recovery process. These losses are not easily recognized, but they are deeply felt. Grieving them allows you to begin the healing journey, rebuilding the pieces of yourself that were taken by the toxic dynamics of workplace bullying. As you move forward, remember that healing is a journey, not a destination, and each step you take toward reclaiming your self-worth, trust, and passion is an act of empowerment. The journey may be long, but it is one that leads to greater emotional safety, personal strength, and peace.

Chapter 5

The Aftermath – Emotional, Physical, and Career Damage

Introduction

The aftermath of workplace bullying and gaslighting can feel like a storm that has ravaged not only your career but also your emotional and physical well-being. The abuse you endured may have been invisible to others, but its effects are profound and far-reaching. When the bullying ends, it doesn't always mean that the damage is over. In fact, the true cost often reveals itself after the toxic environment has been left behind, and the emotional, physical, and career impacts of the abuse become more apparent.

In this chapter, we will explore the emotional toll of workplace bullying and gaslighting, including the often debilitating effects of burnout, depression, and anxiety. We will discuss how these emotional challenges can manifest physically in somatic symptoms like fatigue, illness, and chronic stress. Additionally, we will delve into the career damage caused by the long-term effects of bullying, such as quitting, demotion, or professional stagnation. Finally, we will address the overwhelming feelings of guilt and embarrassment that often accompany this period of recovery, and how to navigate these emotions on the road to healing.

Burnout, Depression, and Anxiety Post-Bullying

The emotional impact of workplace bullying often lingers long after the abusive behavior has stopped. Burnout, depression, and anxiety are common responses to prolonged mistreatment in the workplace, and they can significantly affect an individual's ability to function both personally and professionally.

Burnout: The Emotional Exhaustion

Burnout is one of the most common emotional responses to workplace bullying, particularly when the abuse has been ongoing. It is a state of emotional, physical, and mental exhaustion caused by excessive and prolonged stress. For those who have experienced bullying, burnout may manifest as a complete depletion of energy and motivation. The constant pressure to perform, the emotional toll of being mistreated, and the need to constantly protect oneself from further harm can leave individuals feeling drained and empty.

Signs of burnout include:

- **Exhaustion**: Both physical and emotional fatigue that feels overwhelming and unrelenting.

- **Cynicism**: A sense of hopelessness or detachment from your work, colleagues, or professional goals.

- **Irritability**: Increased frustration and irritability, often triggered by minor events.

- **Difficulty concentrating**: An inability to focus or complete tasks efficiently.

- **Lack of fulfillment**: A sense that work no longer provides any satisfaction or meaning.

Burnout caused by workplace bullying is not just about being tired; it's a profound emotional and psychological toll. The constant stress and lack of support can make individuals feel as if they are incapable of recovering, which only deepens their emotional exhaustion.

Depression: The Weight of Emotional Abuse

Workplace bullying is a significant risk factor for depression. When you are constantly devalued, belittled, and manipulated, it's natural to begin to question your worth and feel like you are trapped in a situation with no escape. The emotional toll of bullying can lead to feelings of sadness, hopelessness, and despair, which are hallmarks of depression.

Depression post-bullying can manifest in several ways:

- **Persistent sadness**: A pervasive sense of sadness or emptiness that doesn't seem to go away.

- **Loss of interest**: A lack of interest in activities that you once enjoyed, including work, socializing, or hobbies.

- **Low self-esteem**: A deep sense of worthlessness or failure, often tied to the demeaning behavior of the bully.

- **Sleep disturbances**: Trouble falling asleep or staying asleep due to anxiety or stress.

- **Difficulty making decisions**: Feeling paralyzed by the inability to make decisions or take action, even on routine tasks.

For many individuals who have been bullied at work, depression becomes a constant companion. The feelings of inadequacy, failure, and the constant questioning of one's abilities can chip away at an individual's mental health, leaving them with little emotional energy to face the day.

Anxiety: The Lingering Fear

Anxiety is another common emotional consequence of workplace bullying. When you've been subjected to bullying, you may find yourself in a constant state of hypervigilance—always on edge, always anticipating the next attack. The fear of further mistreatment or retaliation can be debilitating, leaving individuals unable to relax or feel safe, even in the absence of their abuser.

Signs of anxiety include:

- **Constant worry**: An overwhelming sense of fear or dread, often without a clear cause.

- **Physical symptoms**: Racing heart, shallow breathing, tight muscles, or stomach discomfort.

- **Avoidance behaviors**: Avoiding certain situations, people, or places that remind you of the bullying or make you feel unsafe.

- **Panic attacks**: Sudden, intense episodes of fear or anxiety, accompanied by physical symptoms such as rapid heartbeat, shortness of breath, and dizziness.

Anxiety can be crippling, making it difficult to return to the workplace or even engage in social situations. The emotional toll of workplace bullying often leaves individuals feeling as if they are constantly walking on eggshells, and the fear of being hurt again can prevent them from fully healing.

Somatic Symptoms: Fatigue, Illness, and Chronic Stress

The emotional toll of workplace bullying often manifests physically in the form of somatic symptoms. These are physical symptoms that arise as a result of emotional or psychological stress. Chronic stress, anxiety, and emotional exhaustion from bullying can manifest in a variety of physical ailments, which can further complicate the healing process.

Fatigue

Chronic fatigue is one of the most common physical symptoms experienced by individuals who have been bullied at work. The emotional toll of being constantly undermined, criticized, or isolated drains both your physical and mental energy. Over time, this fatigue becomes pervasive, affecting every aspect of life. Even after a full night's sleep, you may wake up feeling drained and unrefreshed. The constant state of stress and anxiety that accompanies workplace bullying can cause your body to remain in "fight-or-flight" mode, depleting your energy reserves and preventing true rest and recovery.

Illness and Weakened Immune System

Chronic stress from workplace bullying can weaken the immune system, making individuals more susceptible to illness. The stress response increases the production of cortisol, the body's primary stress hormone. Prolonged elevated cortisol levels can lead to a host of physical health problems, including digestive issues, headaches, muscle tension, and a weakened immune system. As a result, you may find yourself becoming ill more frequently, or struggling to recover from common ailments like colds or infections.

Chronic Stress and Its Physical Effects

Chronic stress, anxiety, and emotional turmoil have widespread effects on the body. Beyond fatigue and illness, these stressors can contribute to conditions such as high blood pressure, heart disease, gastrointestinal problems, and sleep disturbances. Over time, the toll of sustained stress on the body can lead to long-term health issues, further complicating recovery from the emotional scars of bullying.

Somatic symptoms are a powerful reminder that emotional and physical health are deeply interconnected. When bullying goes unaddressed, it can lead to a cascade of physical symptoms that prolong the healing process and may even require medical intervention.

Career Detours: Quitting, Demotion, Stalling Out

Workplace bullying and gaslighting often result in career damage that extends well beyond the immediate emotional impact. The toll of sustained mistreatment can cause individuals to make difficult decisions about their careers, such as quitting, accepting demotion, or stalling out professionally.

Quitting: The Escape

For many individuals, quitting the job is the only way to escape the toxic environment of bullying. While quitting may provide immediate relief from the abuse, it can also lead to feelings of failure, shame, or guilt. There may be lingering doubts about whether leaving was the right decision or whether you could have handled the situation differently. Despite these feelings, quitting can often be the healthiest choice for preserving your well-being, as staying in an abusive environment can lead to further emotional and physical damage.

Demotion: Accepting a Reduced Role

In some cases, victims of bullying may accept a demotion as a way to escape direct interaction with their abuser or reduce the stress of their role. While this may seem like a temporary solution, it often leads to long-term dissatisfaction and a sense of being undervalued. A demotion can contribute to feelings of inadequacy and failure, further exacerbating the emotional damage caused by the bullying.

Stalling Out Professionally: Losing Motivation and Ambition

Workplace bullying can also result in career stagnation, where an individual feels "stuck" or unable to progress professionally. The emotional toll of constant mistreatment, coupled with diminished self-esteem and a lack of confidence, can cause individuals to lose their drive and ambition. They may stop pursuing promotions, new opportunities, or career growth, believing that they are no longer capable or worthy of success. This stalling out can have long-term effects on an individual's career trajectory, as they may become trapped in roles that no longer inspire them or align with their skills.

Navigating the Guilt and Embarrassment

One of the most common and insidious emotions experienced by victims of workplace bullying is guilt. Many individuals feel guilty for not speaking up sooner, for not confronting the bully directly, or for "allowing" the mistreatment to continue. This guilt is often compounded by feelings of embarrassment—embarrassment that they were manipulated, humiliated, or emotionally harmed by a colleague or superior. The idea of being "weak" or "too sensitive" is reinforced by the myth that employees should simply tolerate mistreatment as part of the job.

It is important to recognize that these feelings of guilt and embarrassment are a natural response to being bullied, but they do not reflect your worth or your responsibility in the situation. You are not to blame for the behavior of the bully, and you have nothing to be ashamed of for experiencing emotional pain or seeking help. Healing from workplace bullying involves recognizing that you were the victim of manipulative, toxic behavior, and that you deserve to heal and recover without carrying the weight of misplaced guilt.

Conclusion

The aftermath of workplace bullying and gaslighting is far-reaching, touching every aspect of an individual's emotional, physical, and professional life. The effects of burnout, depression, anxiety, and somatic symptoms can be debilitating, leaving individuals feeling as if they are forever trapped in the wake of their abuse. The career damage caused by bullying—whether through quitting, demotion, or professional stagnation—can also create feelings of failure and shame.

However, understanding that these emotional, physical, and career challenges are natural consequences of workplace abuse is the first step in the healing process. Acknowledging the guilt and embarrassment, while challenging and uncomfortable, is also vital for moving forward. Healing requires reclaiming control over your emotional safety, recognizing your worth, and taking steps to rebuild your self-esteem, physical health, and professional confidence. It is a long journey, but one that leads to reclaiming your peace, well-being, and the future you deserve.

Chapter 6

Naming It to Tame It – Language That Sets You Free

Introduction

When we experience trauma, particularly in the form of workplace bullying or gaslighting, we often find ourselves caught in a whirlwind of confusion, self-doubt, and emotional turmoil. The behaviors we endure can be so manipulative and subtle that they leave us questioning our perceptions and wondering if we're simply "too sensitive" or "overreacting." In these moments, one of the most powerful tools we have is language—the ability to name what is happening to us, to articulate our pain, and to take control over the narrative that has been imposed upon us.

Naming our experiences isn't just about giving them a label; it's about finding clarity and reclaiming our power. By putting words to our suffering, we break the silence that has kept us trapped and take the first step toward healing. This chapter is dedicated to helping you create the emotional vocabulary you need to understand and express your experience. We'll explore how naming what has happened to you transforms confusion into clarity and offers a path to emotional freedom. We'll also look at how to break the silence around your abuse without compromising your own well-being and provide you with practical scripts for disclosure, whether to therapists, family members, or friends.

Creating Emotional Vocabulary for Your Experience

One of the most difficult parts of experiencing workplace bullying or gaslighting is the sheer difficulty of identifying and naming what's happening. The gaslighter often distorts reality to the point where you question your own perceptions, leaving you unsure of what to call the emotions or behaviors you're facing. Is it criticism? Manipulation? Abuse? Is it you being overly sensitive, or is there something more insidious happening?

Creating a clear emotional vocabulary is essential for understanding your experience and moving toward healing. Having the right language allows you to:

1. **Acknowledge the Impact**: Naming the emotional toll of your experience enables you to validate your feelings. For example, recognizing that you are suffering from **burnout, anxiety**, or **imposter syndrome** as a result of the bullying can help you understand the extent of the damage.

2. **Identify the Behavior**: When you can name the actions of the bully—whether it's **gaslighting, undermining**, or **passive-aggression**—you gain clarity about what you're facing. These labels not only help you make sense of the situation but also allow you to distance yourself from the manipulation.

3. **Find Empowerment**: Understanding and naming what's happening to you empowers you to take control of your response. Instead of feeling helpless or confused, you can recognize that you are being targeted and that the behaviors you're experiencing are intentional.

4. **Communicate Clearly**: Having the right words allows you to articulate your experience to others in a way that is accurate and unambiguous. Whether you're talking to a therapist, family member, or colleague, using the right language helps you communicate your experience with confidence.

From Confusion to Clarity: The Power of Accurate Naming

One of the most profound benefits of naming your experience is the clarity it brings. When you're in the midst of workplace bullying or gaslighting, everything can feel disorienting. You may feel like you're walking through fog, constantly questioning whether what you're experiencing is real, whether your feelings are justified, or whether you're imagining things. The clarity that comes from naming the behaviors you're facing can help dispel this fog, making it easier to understand what's happening and how to respond.

Gaslighting: Understanding the Manipulation

Gaslighting, a term that has its origins in a 1938 play and subsequent movie *Gaslight*, is a form of psychological manipulation where the abuser causes the victim to question their perception of reality. It involves deliberate distortion of facts, denial of events that have occurred, and even lying to make the victim feel crazy or irrational. Recognizing that you are being gaslit—whether in the form of denying things you've said or twisting the facts—is the first step in regaining control over the situation.

Once you name the behavior as gaslighting, it's easier to identify when it happens and respond accordingly, rather than questioning your own reality. This clarity helps you regain a sense of certainty and stability in your perception.

Bullying: Understanding the Aggression

Workplace bullying can manifest in many ways—through verbal abuse, intimidation, exclusion, undermining, or even sabotage. But all forms of bullying have one thing in common: they are designed to create fear, insecurity, and a sense of powerlessness in the victim. Understanding that what you are experiencing is bullying, and not just part of the "rough and tumble" of work life, is essential for healing. Naming it as such helps you see that it's not about your inability to handle stress or difficult people, but rather the result of a toxic, abusive work environment.

When you recognize bullying for what it is, it's easier to stand firm in your understanding that you deserve to work in a safe, supportive environment—one where you are treated with respect and dignity.

Breaking the Silence Without Breaking Yourself

One of the most difficult aspects of experiencing workplace bullying or gaslighting is the pressure to remain silent. For many victims, speaking out about the abuse is fraught with fear and uncertainty. You may worry about retaliation, being labeled as difficult, or even losing your job. These fears are often compounded by the silence surrounding these issues—bullying and gaslighting are often dismissed as "part of the job" or something to "tough out."

However, breaking the silence is essential for healing and reclaiming your power. That being said, it's important to do so in a way that protects your emotional and mental health. Here are some strategies for breaking the silence without breaking yourself:

1. **Set Boundaries**: Before disclosing your experience, take some time to set clear emotional and personal boundaries. Know what you're comfortable sharing and with whom. It's okay to take a step back if you're not ready to talk about everything right away.

2. **Start with a Trusted Individual**: Disclosing your experience can feel overwhelming, so start with someone you trust—a close friend, family member, or therapist. Share your feelings and experiences in a safe, supportive environment where you feel validated and heard.

3. **Be Strategic in the Workplace**: If you decide to address the bullying within the workplace, it's important to choose the right moment and the right people to talk to. If your manager or HR is part of the problem, you may want to seek out an external

therapist or support group before disclosing anything to the workplace. Sometimes, it's helpful to document your experiences first and present them in writing to minimize emotional exposure.

4. **Avoid Self-Blame**: When you start speaking about your experience, it's easy to fall into the trap of self-blame or apologizing for your feelings. Remind yourself that you are not responsible for the bullying or gaslighting. Your feelings are valid, and you deserve to be treated with respect.

5. **Use Clear, Specific Language**: When you do speak up, use clear and specific language to describe your experience. Instead of saying, "I feel like I'm being treated badly," say, "I have been subjected to persistent verbal insults and criticism in meetings, and this has caused me to feel anxious and unsafe at work." Clear language helps others understand the severity of the situation.

Scripts for Disclosure: Therapists, Family, Friends

The way you disclose your experience can vary depending on who you are speaking with—whether it's a therapist, a family member, or a friend. Having a script in mind can help you feel more in control of the conversation and ensure that your emotions and experiences are communicated clearly.

To a Therapist

When speaking to a therapist, it's important to focus on both the emotional and psychological impact of the bullying. You may start by explaining the specific behaviors you've experienced and how they have affected your mental health.

Example script:

"I've been dealing with a situation at work where I've been constantly undermined and criticized by a colleague. At first, I thought it was just part of the job, but it's become overwhelming. I feel anxious all the time, and I've started questioning my abilities. I'm not sure how to deal with the emotional toll it's taking on me. Can you help me process this?"

To Family

Family members may be more emotionally invested in your well-being, so it's important to share your experience without overloading them with details that could increase their anxiety. Focus on how the bullying is affecting your overall well-being.

Example script:

"I want to talk to you about something that's been happening at work. I've been dealing with a difficult situation where I've been treated unfairly and made to feel less than capable. It's been affecting my mental health, and I'm struggling with how to handle it. I just need someone to listen and help me figure out what to do next."

To Friends

When talking to friends, you may want to lean on their support and validation. Share your experience and ask for their emotional support without over-explaining every detail.

Example script:

"I've been going through a really tough time at work. I've been dealing with a toxic situation where I've been treated badly, and it's really starting to affect me. I need your support as I figure out how to handle it. I just wanted to share this with you because it's been weighing on me."

Conclusion

Naming your experience of workplace bullying and gaslighting is the first step toward healing. Creating a vocabulary that accurately captures the emotional and psychological impact of these experiences allows you to reclaim control over your story. It transforms confusion into clarity and empowers you to speak your truth without fear or shame. Breaking the silence is essential for recovery, but it is important to do so in a way that protects your emotional well-being. By using clear, specific language and reaching out to trusted individuals—whether it's a therapist, family member, or friend—you can begin the process of healing and reclaim your confidence. Naming it truly helps to tame it, and in doing so, you take the first step in reclaiming your peace, power, and sense of self.

Chapter 7

Boundaries, Baby – Learning Emotional Safety All Over Again

Introduction

For those who have experienced workplace bullying and gaslighting, setting boundaries may feel like an insurmountable challenge. After being manipulated, belittled, or controlled, it's easy to feel like your personal boundaries have been shattered or trampled upon. You might find yourself unsure of where your limits are, how to protect your emotional space, or even how to assert your needs without feeling overwhelmed by guilt or fear.

Learning to rebuild boundaries—both in and outside of the workplace—is a crucial part of healing and reclaiming your emotional safety. Boundaries are not about erecting walls that keep people out; they are about understanding where you end and someone else begins. They define what is acceptable to you, what is not, and how you can protect yourself from further harm without isolating yourself from others.

In this chapter, we'll explore how to rebuild boundaries after trauma, including how to differentiate between fear-based walls and healthy, empowering limits. We'll talk about the essential skill of saying "no" without feeling panic or guilt, and how to identify red flags early on in future relationships—whether at work or in your personal life. Setting boundaries is an ongoing practice, but it is one of the most effective tools for protecting your emotional well-being and ensuring that you never allow anyone to cross your limits again.

Rebuilding Boundaries In and Out of Work

After experiencing workplace bullying or gaslighting, your ability to establish and maintain healthy boundaries may have been deeply affected. Emotional boundaries are not something that can be fixed overnight. They require reflection, practice, and sometimes, an entire reframe of how you perceive your own worth and needs.

Identifying Your Emotional Needs

The first step in rebuilding boundaries is understanding your emotional needs. Many individuals who have experienced bullying or gaslighting often lose sight of these needs because their personal space has been invaded for so long. The bullying may have led you to doubt what you need or feel entitled to, making it difficult to know where to begin.

Start by asking yourself key questions:

- What makes me feel safe and respected?

- What type of behavior from others do I find unacceptable?

- What does emotional safety look like for me in my work and personal life?

Answering these questions will help you clarify what your boundaries are and where you need to start protecting yourself. It's important to recognize that you are deserving of emotional safety and respect—no one has the right to make you feel small, unimportant, or invisible. Once you identify what you need, it becomes easier to articulate those needs to others and start setting the boundaries necessary to honor your emotional space.

Boundaries at Work

Setting boundaries at work can be one of the most challenging aspects of recovery, especially if your previous work environment was toxic or abusive. In these environments, the line between personal space and professional expectations can easily become blurred. You may have felt pressure to overextend yourself, sacrifice your personal time, or tolerate inappropriate behavior for the sake of your job or career advancement.

Rebuilding your work boundaries begins by recognizing that your well-being should never be sacrificed for the sake of work. This involves setting clear limits on what you are willing to tolerate and what you will no longer accept.

Some strategies for rebuilding work boundaries include:

- **Limiting work hours**: If you've been conditioned to work long hours, start by setting specific times when your workday ends. Make it clear that after these hours, you are unavailable for work-related issues unless absolutely necessary.

- **Creating a communication framework**: Decide how you want to communicate with your colleagues and managers. Setting expectations around your availability, preferred methods of communication, and your personal time helps establish your boundaries and reduces emotional stress.

- **Saying "no" to unreasonable requests**: If a colleague or boss asks you to take on additional tasks or responsibilities that you don't have the bandwidth for, practice saying "no." Politely but firmly refuse to take on tasks that compromise your mental health or violate your personal boundaries.

- **Requesting respect**: If you encounter disrespectful behavior or undermining, speak up for yourself. You don't have to tolerate bullying, manipulation, or passive-aggressive behavior. Assert yourself calmly but confidently, and make it clear that such behavior will not be tolerated.

Boundaries in Your Personal Life

While work boundaries are crucial for protecting yourself from toxic environments, boundaries in your personal life are just as important. After experiencing emotional abuse, you may find it difficult to trust others or be unsure of how much emotional vulnerability is safe. However, learning to set healthy boundaries in personal relationships is key to maintaining your emotional safety and self-worth.

Setting boundaries in your personal life can involve:

- **Recognizing toxic relationships**: If you have friends, family members, or romantic partners who undermine or manipulate you, it may be time to set boundaries with them. Don't feel obligated to maintain relationships that are emotionally draining or abusive.

- **Saying "no" to overcommitment**: Many individuals who have experienced bullying or gaslighting feel the need to please others or say "yes" to every request in an attempt to avoid conflict or gain approval. Begin saying "no" to commitments that don't serve you or respect your time and energy.

- **Prioritizing self-care**: Your emotional well-being should be a priority. Make time for activities that nurture your body and mind—whether it's spending time with loved ones, engaging in a hobby, or simply resting. These acts of self-care reinforce your boundaries and remind you of your worth.

Understanding the Difference Between Fear Walls and Healthy Limits

As you rebuild boundaries, it's essential to differentiate between healthy, empowered boundaries and fear-based walls. Fear walls are an instinctive reaction to past harm, designed to protect you from further emotional damage. However, these walls are not always healthy—they can isolate you from others and prevent you from engaging in meaningful relationships.

Fear Walls:

Fear walls are defensive mechanisms built from past trauma. These walls are created to protect you from further harm, but they can also prevent growth and connection. You may set these walls as a way of keeping everyone at arm's length, avoiding any potential threat to your emotional safety.

Examples of fear walls include:

- **Emotional withdrawal**: Shutting yourself off from others to avoid getting hurt.

- **Overgeneralizing**: Assuming that all people are untrustworthy or abusive based on past experiences.

- **Avoiding confrontation**: Refusing to speak up or assert yourself because you fear retaliation or further manipulation.

While fear walls may provide a temporary sense of safety, they ultimately limit your ability to build meaningful connections, both at work and in your personal life.

Healthy Limits:

Healthy limits, on the other hand, are boundaries that come from a place of self-respect and self-love. Healthy boundaries are not designed to isolate you but to protect you and ensure that your needs are met in a way that respects your autonomy and emotional safety. Healthy boundaries allow you to engage with others without compromising your sense of self or emotional well-being.

Examples of healthy limits include:

- **Clear communication**: Expressing your needs and desires honestly and respectfully without fear of judgment.

- **Self-respect**: Prioritizing your own well-being and making choices that align with your values and boundaries.

- **Openness to vulnerability**: Allowing yourself to connect with others while maintaining the strength to set limits when necessary.

Healthy limits are flexible, empowering, and designed to foster connection and mutual respect. They allow you to protect your emotional well-being while still engaging meaningfully with others.

Saying "No" Without Panic or Guilt

One of the most challenging aspects of rebuilding boundaries after workplace bullying or gaslighting is learning to say "no" without feeling panic or guilt. For many people, saying "no" feels like an insurmountable hurdle—especially if they've been conditioned to please others or avoid conflict. But saying "no" is an essential part of boundary-setting and is crucial for maintaining emotional safety.

To say "no" without guilt:

1. **Understand that "no" is a complete sentence**: You don't need to justify or over-explain your boundaries. A simple, respectful "no" is enough.

2. **Practice self-compassion**: Recognize that saying "no" is an act of self-care, not selfishness. You have the right to protect your time, energy, and emotional well-being.

3. **Use assertive language**: Practice saying "no" with confidence. For example, "I'm unable to take on additional work at this time" or "That's not something I'm willing to do."

4. **Be firm but polite**: You can say "no" firmly without being rude or defensive. It's about protecting your needs while maintaining respect for the other person.

The more you practice saying "no" in small, everyday situations, the easier it will become to assert your boundaries without fear or guilt.

How to Spot Red Flags Early Next Time

As you rebuild your emotional boundaries, it's important to develop the skill of recognizing red flags early in future relationships—whether at work or in your personal life. The sooner you can spot toxic behaviors, the sooner you can take steps to protect yourself.

Some common red flags include:

- **Excessive criticism**: If someone constantly undermines you or makes you feel less than, it's a sign of unhealthy dynamics.

- **Manipulation or gaslighting**: If someone tries to make you doubt your reality or consistently denies things that you know are true, trust your instincts.

- **Lack of respect for your time**: If others regularly disrespect your personal boundaries—whether it's demanding your time, interrupting your personal space, or overstepping your limits— this is a red flag.

- **Unwarranted guilt-tripping**: If someone tries to make you feel guilty for setting boundaries or saying "no," they are not respecting your emotional safety.

Trust your intuition when you encounter these red flags. Setting boundaries early on can prevent toxic behavior from taking root in your life.

Conclusion

Rebuilding emotional boundaries after workplace bullying or gaslighting is a journey of reclaiming your power, your identity, and your well-being. Learning to recognize and establish healthy boundaries—both in work and personal life—empowers you to protect yourself and honor your emotional needs. By differentiating between fear walls and healthy limits, you can establish a foundation of self-respect that allows for genuine connections and growth. Learning to say "no" without guilt and recognizing red flags early on will ensure that you no longer tolerate toxic behavior, allowing you to move forward with confidence and emotional safety. Setting boundaries is not only a way to protect yourself; it is an act of self-love, and a crucial step on the road to recovery.

Chapter 8

The Voice You Forgot You Had – Reclaiming Your Confidence

Introduction

After experiencing workplace bullying and gaslighting, it's common for individuals to lose their confidence. The constant undermining, criticism, and manipulation can silence the voice you once had, leaving you questioning your worth, abilities, and sense of self. The emotional scars of bullying can make you feel small, invisible, and powerless, and over time, you may forget what it feels like to trust yourself or believe in your own value.

But reclaiming your confidence is possible. It's not about becoming louder or more forceful; it's about rediscovering your inner strength and learning to trust yourself again. Confidence isn't something that can be forced—it is something that grows steadily, over time, through consistent practice, small victories, and the gradual process of rebuilding your sense of self-worth. In this chapter, we'll explore how bullying silences your voice, how to rebuild self-trust through tiny wins, and why true confidence is not loud but steady. We'll also address how to talk back to your inner critic—the voice that often mimics your bully—and replace it with self-compassion and belief in your own strength.

What Bullying Silences (And How to Reclaim It)

Workplace bullying and gaslighting are not just about the external harm they cause—they are deeply internalized, leaving lasting effects on how you perceive yourself. One of the most profound impacts of bullying is that it silences your voice. Not just the literal voice of speaking up or expressing your thoughts, but the metaphorical voice of confidence, self-expression, and self-advocacy.

Silencing Your Voice of Self-Worth

Bullies thrive on diminishing others. They do this by belittling your accomplishments, making you doubt your abilities, and making you feel undeserving of respect. Over time, the consistent undermining of your worth can cause you to internalize these criticisms, silencing the voice inside you that says, "I am enough." Your achievements, ideas, and opinions may begin to feel unimportant or unworthy of being expressed, and the silence becomes a defense mechanism.

The first step in reclaiming your confidence is recognizing what bullying has taken from you. Your voice is an essential part of your identity. It represents your ideas, your values, your needs, and your emotions. When that voice is silenced, it's easy to lose sight of who you are. Reclaiming your voice begins by acknowledging that you are worthy of being heard. Your thoughts and feelings are valid, and you have the right to express them without fear of judgment or retaliation.

Reclaiming Your Voice: Speak Your Truth

Reclaiming your voice means learning to speak your truth, even in the face of doubt. It doesn't mean you have to shout from the rooftops, but it does mean that you recognize the power of your words and the importance of asserting yourself.

Start by:

1. **Identifying Your Truths**: Reflect on what you believe about yourself, your worth, and your abilities. What are the things that you've been afraid to say because you felt silenced or diminished by others? Start with small affirmations—"I am worthy," "I deserve respect," "My voice matters."

2. **Speaking Up in Small Ways**: Reclaiming your voice is a gradual process. Start with small instances where you can assert your needs or express your opinions. This could be in conversations with friends, family, or colleagues where you feel safe. The more you speak up, the more you'll reinforce your sense of self and your ability to be heard.

3. **Creating Safe Spaces for Expression**: Whether it's through journaling, art, or simply having conversations with trusted friends, find ways to express yourself freely. The act of sharing your thoughts in any form is a powerful step in reclaiming your voice.

Rebuilding Self-Trust: Tiny Wins and Personal Truths

Self-trust is the foundation of confidence. When you've been the target of bullying, particularly gaslighting, your ability to trust yourself is often eroded. The repeated questioning of your thoughts, feelings, and perceptions can lead you to doubt everything, including your judgment and instincts. Rebuilding self-trust is a critical part of restoring your confidence, but it is a process that takes time and patience.

Tiny Wins: Building Confidence One Step at a Time

Rebuilding self-trust doesn't happen all at once. It's built gradually, through small actions and consistent practice. Tiny wins, those little moments where you assert yourself, make a decision, or take a step outside of your comfort zone, are key to rebuilding trust in yourself.

Here's how you can start:

1. **Set Achievable Goals**: Begin with small, achievable goals that you know you can accomplish. These goals don't need to be monumental—starting with something simple, like voicing an opinion in a meeting or setting a healthy boundary with a colleague, can be incredibly empowering. Each time you achieve a goal, no matter how small, you reinforce your self-trust.

2. **Celebrate Every Step**: Acknowledge and celebrate every step of progress, no matter how small it seems. Whether it's standing up for yourself, making a decision, or confronting a difficult situation, recognize that each action contributes to rebuilding your confidence and trust in yourself.

3. **Practice Self-Compassion**: Rebuilding self-trust also means being compassionate with yourself. Recognize that there will be setbacks, that rebuilding takes time, and that it's okay to make mistakes along the way. Instead of harshly criticizing yourself for moments of doubt or failure, treat yourself with kindness and understanding. This self-compassion builds trust in your ability to handle challenges without being too hard on yourself.

4. **Align with Personal Truths**: Rebuilding trust also means reconnecting with your core values and truths. What do you believe about yourself and the world around you? What are your passions and goals? Trusting yourself means aligning your actions with your personal truths, even when fear or doubt arise.

Confidence Isn't Loud – It's Steady

Many people mistakenly associate confidence with loudness, assertiveness, or forcefulness. In reality, confidence is not about dominating conversations or proving your worth through external achievements. True confidence comes from within—it's steady, quiet, and unwavering. Confidence is about having the internal strength to remain grounded and true to yourself, even when the world around you is chaotic or dismissive.

The Quiet Strength of Confidence

True confidence is not about seeking external validation or approval—it's about accepting and trusting yourself, regardless of what others think or say. It is a quiet, steadfast belief that you are enough, just as you are.

Here are some key aspects of steady confidence:

1. **Self-Awareness**: Confidence begins with a deep understanding of who you are—your values, your strengths, and your limitations. When you know and accept yourself, it becomes easier to stand firm in your confidence, without the need for external validation.

2. **Self-Acceptance**: True confidence comes from accepting yourself with all your flaws and imperfections. Instead of striving for perfection, confident people embrace their humanity and imperfections. They understand that mistakes and failures are part of the journey, and they don't define their worth.

3. **Resilience**: Confidence is also about resilience—the ability to bounce back after setbacks, learn from mistakes, and keep moving forward. Confident individuals are not immune to challenges, but they have the inner strength to navigate them with grace and perseverance.

4. **Calm Assertiveness**: Confidence doesn't need to be loud. It's about being able to assert your needs and opinions calmly and clearly, without being aggressive or defensive. Confident people know their worth and can communicate it without hesitation, but they don't need to shout to be heard.

Talking Back to Your Inner Critic (Which Often Mimics Your Bully)

One of the most challenging aspects of regaining confidence is confronting the inner critic—the voice in your head that echoes the harsh words and criticism of the bully. After being subjected to bullying, your inner voice may sound eerily similar to the voice of your abuser, repeating negative thoughts like "You're not good enough" or "You'll never succeed."

The Inner Critic: Recognizing the Damage

The inner critic is a product of internalized negative beliefs. It's the voice that tells you you're unworthy, unqualified, or undeserving of success. It often mirrors the words of the bully and is designed to undermine your confidence and keep you small.

Talking Back to Your Inner Critic

To reclaim your confidence, you must challenge the inner critic and replace those negative, self-sabotaging thoughts with positive, affirming ones. Here's how you can begin:

1. **Recognize the Critic**: The first step is recognizing when your inner critic is speaking. Pay attention to the thoughts that arise when you're facing challenges or making decisions. Are they rooted in fear or self-doubt? Are they echoing the words of your abuser? Once you can identify these thoughts, you can begin to counter them.

2. **Challenge Negative Beliefs**: When your inner critic tells you that you're not good enough or that you can't succeed, challenge those beliefs with evidence to the contrary. Remind yourself of your achievements, strengths, and past successes. Replace "I can't" with "I can" or "I'm learning."

3. **Reframe Negative Thoughts**: Reframing is a powerful tool in combating the inner critic. When negative thoughts arise, try to reframe them in a positive light. For example, instead of thinking, "I always fail at this," reframe it as, "I may not have succeeded this time, but I am learning and improving."

4. **Practice Self-Affirmations**: Use positive affirmations to counteract the negative voice in your head. Write down affirmations that remind you of your worth, strength, and potential. Repeat these affirmations daily to reinforce a positive self-image.

Conclusion

Reclaiming your confidence after workplace bullying and gaslighting is a journey of rediscovering your inner strength, trust, and self-worth. Confidence is not about being loud or forceful—it is about being steady, grounded, and true to yourself. By learning to rebuild your boundaries, challenge the inner critic, and trust in your own abilities, you can slowly but surely regain your confidence. It takes time, patience, and practice, but with each step you take, you'll find yourself becoming more resilient, self-assured, and empowered. Your voice is still there—it was never lost.

Now it's time to reclaim it, and in doing so, reclaim the confidence that belongs to you.

Chapter 9

Emotional Detox – Releasing the Gaslighting Residue

Introduction

Healing from workplace bullying and gaslighting is no easy task. The long-term emotional toll often leaves behind what I call "gaslighting residue"—the lingering effects of manipulation that warp your perception of reality, your sense of self-worth, and your emotional well-being. Gaslighting is a form of psychological manipulation where the victim is made to question their perceptions, memories, and sense of reality. Over time, this emotional abuse can cause deep confusion and cognitive dissonance, leaving individuals feeling uncertain about their own thoughts and emotions.

In this chapter, we will explore the process of emotional detox—how to release the lingering effects of gaslighting and begin healing from the confusion, self-doubt, and emotional turmoil it causes. We will focus on understanding cognitive dissonance and how to heal from it, as well as addressing the common question "Did I imagine it?" (No, you didn't). We will also discuss how to reprogram internalized gaslighting and offer practical tools such as journal prompts, affirmations, and emotional grounding practices to help you regain your emotional clarity and strength. Through this emotional detox, you will learn how to free yourself from the residue of gaslighting and reclaim your truth.

Healing from Cognitive Dissonance

Cognitive dissonance occurs when there is a significant conflict between our beliefs, values, or perceptions and the reality we are presented with. It's the psychological discomfort we feel when we are confronted with information or experiences that challenge what we've always believed to be true. In the case of workplace bullying and gaslighting, cognitive dissonance manifests when the victim's perception of reality is constantly challenged by the abuser's manipulations.

What is Cognitive Dissonance in the Context of Gaslighting?

Gaslighting is a powerful tool of psychological manipulation that distorts reality and causes confusion. A classic example is when the abuser denies things they've said or done, causing the victim to doubt their own memory. Over time, this repeated distortion creates cognitive dissonance, as the victim is left struggling to reconcile their own perceptions with the abuser's version of events. The emotional toll is severe because the victim starts to believe that they are somehow wrong or crazy for trusting their own senses and experiences.

For example, a gaslighter might say, "That never happened. You're imagining things," even though you clearly remember the event. After repeated exposure to such manipulation, you might start to question your memory or wonder if you're misinterpreting things. This doubt and confusion are at the heart of cognitive dissonance: the tension between what you know to be true in your gut and the conflicting message your abuser is giving you.

The dissonance creates a mental tug-of-war between your internal truth and the external lies being imposed upon you. This constant tension can be exhausting, leaving you emotionally drained, uncertain, and vulnerable.

Healing from Cognitive Dissonance

The healing process begins with recognizing and acknowledging the dissonance you are experiencing. Understanding that the conflict between your inner truth and the manipulative behavior you've endured is a direct result of gaslighting helps you disentangle your reality from the false narrative that has been imposed upon you. Healing from cognitive dissonance involves a few key steps:

1. **Validate Your Perceptions**: One of the first steps to healing from cognitive dissonance is to stop doubting yourself. When gaslighting leads you to question your own experiences, it is crucial to re-establish trust in your perceptions. Remind yourself that your feelings, memories, and observations are valid. They are your reality, and they matter.

2. **Reaffirm Your Truth**: Cognitive dissonance is so powerful because it creates doubt in your own truth. Over time, this leads you to believe that maybe you were wrong to feel a certain way. The antidote to this is reaffirming your own truth. Reconnect

with your personal beliefs and values, and reflect on the times when you've trusted your instincts and been right. Recognize that you have the right to trust your experiences, regardless of what others may have told you.

3. **Challenge the Lies**: Gaslighters thrive on making you doubt your version of events. In order to heal from cognitive dissonance, it is important to challenge the lies that were imposed upon you. Start by recognizing the patterns of manipulation: when they deny things that happened, when they twist the truth, when they make you feel like you're crazy for questioning them. By identifying these tactics, you can reclaim the narrative and affirm your own reality.

4. **Forgive Yourself**: Cognitive dissonance can leave you feeling guilty for questioning yourself, but it's important to understand that this confusion was not your fault. The gaslighter is the one who caused the dissonance, not you. Practice self-compassion and forgive yourself for being manipulated. It's normal to have doubts and confusion when you're constantly exposed to someone who deliberately distorts your reality. Give yourself permission to heal.

"Did I Imagine It?" – No, You Didn't

One of the most common questions victims of gaslighting ask themselves is, "Did I imagine it?" This doubt is a direct result of the gaslighting process. The abuser intentionally creates confusion and uncertainty, causing the victim to question whether they've misinterpreted the situation or whether their emotional responses are exaggerated.

The Gaslighting Cycle of Doubt

Gaslighting is designed to make you feel like your reality is distorted or invalid. The gaslighter may deny events, manipulate conversations, or make you feel crazy for simply expressing your feelings. Over time, this continuous pattern of distortion creates a mental fog that leaves you questioning yourself. The emotional and psychological impact of this manipulation can lead you to believe that you are imagining things or making a big deal out of nothing.

This kind of doubt is not only frustrating—it's destabilizing. When you begin to question whether what you experienced was real, it can feel like you're losing your sense of self. The more you try to make sense of the situation, the more confused and unsure you become. It's easy to fall into the trap of believing that maybe you are overreacting or that you're just being too sensitive.

Affirming the Truth: You Didn't Imagine It

It's essential to remind yourself that what you experienced was real. Gaslighting is not about your emotional sensitivity—it's about manipulation. The events, the emotions, and the mistreatment you faced were real, and your perception of them is valid. Understanding this truth is a critical part of the healing process.

Here are a few steps to help you release the lingering doubt:

1. **Write It Down**: Start keeping a journal where you document your experiences and emotions. Write down instances of gaslighting, bullying, or manipulation as they occur. Over time, you'll have a concrete record of events that can help you recognize patterns and affirm your own reality.

2. **Seek Validation from Trusted Sources**: Talk to people you trust, such as friends, family, or a therapist. Often, a supportive listener can offer a clear perspective and validate your experiences. Reaching out to others who can provide reassurance can help counter the confusion caused by gaslighting.

3. **Reaffirm Your Experiences**: Remind yourself that your feelings and perceptions are not "imagined" or "exaggerated." Trust that your emotions are valid, and honor them. The pain you felt was a natural response to mistreatment, not an overreaction. You are entitled to your emotional truth.

Reprogramming Internalized Gaslighting

One of the most insidious effects of gaslighting is the way it becomes internalized. Over time, the messages you receive from the gaslighter begin to take root in your own mind. You may start to believe their lies, even if you know deep down that something isn't right. These internalized gaslighting messages can manifest as self-doubt, insecurity, and feelings of unworthiness, all of which reinforce the damage done by the abuser.

How Gaslighting Becomes Internalized

Gaslighters use tactics like denial, manipulation, and distortion to wear down your sense of reality. Over time, you start to internalize the abuser's voice. It becomes easier to dismiss your own feelings, doubts, and experiences as invalid or wrong. You may begin to believe the lies they told you—that you're "too sensitive," "crazy," or "ungrateful" for speaking up. This internalized voice of the gaslighter can be louder than your own, making it difficult to trust yourself and your own judgment.

Reprogramming Your Inner Dialogue

To heal from internalized gaslighting, it's important to reprogram your inner dialogue and replace the gaslighter's voice with your own truth. This process takes time and effort, but it is a vital part of reclaiming your confidence and emotional safety.

1. **Acknowledge the Internalized Voice**: The first step in reprogramming is to acknowledge the voice of the gaslighter within. When you hear yourself thinking "I'm not good enough" or "Maybe I'm overreacting," recognize that these thoughts are not your own. They are the echoes of the gaslighter's manipulation. Acknowledge them without judgment.

2. **Challenge Negative Beliefs**: Once you identify the internalized voice, challenge it. Ask yourself, "Is this belief true? Is this how I truly feel, or is it what I've been made to believe?" Replace negative self-talk with affirmations that reflect your true worth and value.

3. **Reaffirm Your Boundaries**: Gaslighting often involves violating your emotional boundaries. As you reprogram your inner dialogue, also take steps to reaffirm your personal boundaries. Be clear with yourself about what is acceptable and what is not. Practicing self-compassion and maintaining boundaries will reinforce the belief that you deserve respect and emotional safety.

4. **Use Positive Affirmations**: Daily affirmations can help break the cycle of negative self-talk. Repeating affirmations such as "I am worthy of love and respect," "My feelings are valid," and "I trust my instincts" can help you replace the gaslighter's voice with your own positive beliefs.

Journal Prompts, Affirmations, and Emotional Grounding Practices

As you go through the process of emotional detox, incorporating journal prompts, affirmations, and grounding practices into your daily routine can help you stay focused on your healing journey.

Journal Prompts

Journaling is a powerful tool for self-reflection and healing. Here are some journal prompts to help you process your experiences and reclaim your truth:

- What is one experience where you felt gaslighted or manipulated at work? How did it make you feel?

- What are some of the lies you've been told by others, and how have you internalized them?

- What positive qualities do you possess that were never acknowledged by the abuser?

- When was the last time you trusted your instincts and felt confident in your judgment? What did that feel like?

- What do you need to let go of in order to heal from the gaslighting you experienced?

Affirmations

Affirmations can help you replace the internalized negativity with self-compassion and confidence. Here are some affirmations to guide your healing:

- "I am worthy of respect and kindness."

- "My feelings are valid, and I trust my instincts."

- "I am not defined by the manipulation of others."

- "I have the power to reclaim my truth."

- "I release all doubt and embrace my inner strength."

Emotional Grounding Practices

Grounding practices help you stay connected to the present moment and your own sense of safety. Here are some techniques to help you ground yourself emotionally:

- **Deep Breathing**: Focus on your breath, inhaling deeply through your nose and exhaling slowly through your mouth. This practice can help calm your nervous system and bring you back to the present.

- **Body Scan**: Take a few moments to check in with your body, starting from your toes and moving up to your head. Pay attention to areas of tension and consciously release it.

- **Mindfulness**: Engage in mindfulness activities like walking in nature or listening to soothing music. This can help you connect with the present moment and create emotional space away from the chaos of gaslighting.

Conclusion

The emotional detox from gaslighting is a gradual but incredibly powerful process. By understanding cognitive dissonance, acknowledging that you did not imagine the abuse, and reprogramming internalized gaslighting, you begin to free yourself from the lingering effects of manipulation. Through journal prompts, affirmations, and grounding practices, you can reconnect with your inner truth, rebuild self-trust, and regain emotional clarity. This detox process is an essential part of healing, allowing you to reclaim your power, voice, and confidence. The more you practice these tools, the more you will feel grounded, strong, and capable of moving forward with a renewed sense of self.

Chapter 10

Community is Medicine – Finding Allies and Support

Introduction

Recovering from workplace bullying and gaslighting can be a profoundly isolating experience. The trauma often leaves you feeling alone, questioning your reality, and unsure of where to turn for help. One of the most healing and transformative steps in this journey is finding a supportive community—people who not only believe your story but also provide the emotional validation and practical guidance needed to heal and rebuild your sense of self.

In this chapter, we'll explore the power of community as a form of emotional medicine. We'll discuss how shared stories and safe spaces can provide the healing connection needed to combat the isolation that comes with trauma. We'll also examine what true support looks like, including the roles that therapists, coaches, and peer groups can play in your recovery process. Finally, we'll talk about the importance of rebuilding relational trust at your own pace and how to navigate the sometimes tricky waters of reconnecting with others after being emotionally harmed.

The Power of Shared Stories and Safe Spaces

One of the most healing aspects of community is the power of shared stories. When you've been through the experience of bullying or gaslighting, it can feel like your reality is unique or that no one will understand what you've been through. This isolation only deepens the emotional wounds. However, finding others who have experienced similar pain can be incredibly validating. When we share our stories in safe spaces, we not only release the burden of carrying our pain alone, but we also find solidarity, understanding, and healing.

The Healing Power of Connection

There is a unique power in knowing that others have walked a similar path. Sharing your story with someone who understands—whether it's a friend, a fellow survivor, or a therapist—can help you process your experience in a way that is impossible when you are alone. When someone listens to you without judgment, it affirms that your feelings are real and valid. This connection is crucial because, during the period of gaslighting and bullying, your emotions were often invalidated or dismissed. Reconnecting with others who genuinely understand is an essential part of healing.

Finding Safe Spaces

A safe space is one where you can share your story, express your feelings, and find understanding without fear of judgment, retaliation, or shame. Safe spaces allow you to be vulnerable and authentic, something that may have been impossible in the abusive environment of a toxic workplace. Whether these spaces are physical, like support groups, or virtual, like online forums or social media communities, they are essential for recovery.

You can find safe spaces by:

- **Seeking out peer support groups**: Many organizations and online communities exist for survivors of workplace bullying and emotional abuse. These spaces allow for honest, empathetic conversations with people who understand the pain you've experienced.

- **Joining therapy groups**: Some therapists offer group therapy sessions where you can share experiences with others who are healing from similar emotional trauma. These sessions are often structured and led by a professional to ensure a safe and supportive environment.

- **Finding trusted allies**: Supportive friends or family members can also be safe spaces. These individuals should be non-judgmental, understanding, and willing to listen without offering unsolicited advice or trying to "fix" the situation.

In these spaces, you can feel the power of collective healing, realizing that you are not alone and that there are others who have not only survived but thrived after experiencing similar abuse.

What Real Support Looks Like (And How to Find It)

Support is a critical element of the recovery process, but it's important to understand what real support looks like. True support is not about offering platitudes or trying to "fix" the problem; it's about empathy, understanding, and providing practical tools to help you move forward. After experiencing bullying and gaslighting, you need more than surface-level help. You need deep, meaningful support that acknowledges your trauma and helps you heal.

Characteristics of Real Support

1. **Validation**: Real support begins with validation. The people who support you should listen to your experience and believe you. Gaslighting, by its nature, distorts your sense of reality, so having someone tell you that your feelings are real and your experiences are valid is a crucial first step in healing.

2. **Empathy**: True support comes from people who genuinely care about your well-being and can empathize with your pain. They don't minimize your experience or tell you to "just move on." Instead, they offer a space where you can grieve, process, and heal at your own pace.

3. **Boundaries**: Healthy support comes from people who respect your emotional boundaries. They know when to give space and when to offer comfort. They understand that your healing process is personal and that it's okay to not always have the answers.

4. **Practical Guidance**: Real support also involves offering practical guidance and resources. This can come in the form of recommending a therapist, providing information about

workplace rights, or helping you find a community that can offer further support.

How to Find Real Support

Finding real support can feel like a daunting task, especially after being manipulated and isolated for so long. But there are many places where you can seek out this kind of healing connection:

1. **Therapists and Coaches**: Mental health professionals such as therapists and coaches are invaluable for processing trauma and offering coping strategies. Therapists can help you unpack the emotional wounds caused by bullying and gaslighting, while coaches can guide you through rebuilding your confidence and reclaiming your personal power.

2. **Peer Support Groups**: As mentioned earlier, peer support groups are essential for finding real support. These groups offer a safe space to connect with others who are going through or have gone through similar experiences. Many groups are moderated by professionals to ensure a healthy environment, and some are focused specifically on workplace bullying or gaslighting survivors.

3. **Online Communities**: Online forums, social media groups, and websites can be a great way to find virtual support. Platforms such as Reddit, Facebook, and specialized websites host communities where you can share your experiences and learn from others who have been in your shoes.

4. **Trusted Friends and Family**: It's important to have people in your life who believe in you and support your healing. These individuals should be willing to listen, offer encouragement, and provide practical assistance as needed. It may take time to rebuild relationships after the trauma of bullying, but it's worth taking the necessary steps to surround yourself with people who genuinely care.

Therapists, Coaches, and Peer Groups

Finding the right type of support is critical for emotional healing. While many survivors benefit from individual therapy, there are also other forms of support that may be useful, such as coaching or peer groups. Let's explore the benefits of each and how to find the right fit for you.

Therapists

Therapists who specialize in trauma recovery are essential in healing from the effects of bullying and gaslighting. A therapist can help you navigate complex emotions, process trauma, and develop healthy coping mechanisms. When searching for a therapist, consider the following:

- **Specialization**: Look for therapists who specialize in trauma recovery or who have experience working with workplace abuse and emotional manipulation.

- **Therapeutic Approach**: Different therapists use different therapeutic approaches, such as Cognitive Behavioral Therapy

(CBT), trauma-informed therapy, or psychodynamic therapy. Research and find the approach that resonates with you.

- **Comfort and Trust**: A key factor in finding a good therapist is feeling comfortable and safe. Trust your instincts about whether you feel heard, understood, and validated by the therapist.

Coaches

While therapists focus on healing emotional trauma, life coaches specialize in helping you rebuild confidence, set goals, and move forward. Coaching can be particularly helpful if you are focused on personal development and reclaiming your power. Coaches can help you:

- **Set Boundaries**: Learning how to assertively set boundaries in all areas of your life is a key focus of coaching.

- **Rebuild Confidence**: Coaches can offer strategies to rebuild your self-esteem, reclaim your personal power, and develop resilience.

- **Define Your Goals**: Coaches can help you clarify what you want out of your career, relationships, and life and create actionable steps to achieve your goals.

Look for coaches who have experience working with people who have been through workplace trauma or bullying. Their experience will help you feel understood and supported in your recovery process.

Peer Support Groups

Peer support groups provide a unique form of emotional healing by offering a safe space to connect with others who understand exactly what you've been through. These groups are often moderated by trained professionals but are based on the experience of the participants. Peer groups can:

- **Offer Emotional Support**: Sharing your experience with others who have been through similar situations creates a sense of connection and validation.

- **Provide Coping Strategies**: Peer support groups often provide practical advice for navigating the emotional aftermath of bullying, such as managing anxiety or rebuilding confidence.

- **Create a Sense of Belonging**: These groups offer a community where you can feel understood and accepted, reducing feelings of isolation.

Peer support groups can be found online, in therapy settings, or through local organizations focused on workplace rights and mental health.

Rebuilding Relational Trust at Your Own Pace

One of the most difficult aspects of healing from bullying and gaslighting is rebuilding relational trust. When you've been manipulated and betrayed by someone in a position of power, it can be difficult to trust anyone—whether in your professional or personal life. This lack of trust can extend beyond the workplace, affecting your ability to form meaningful connections with others.

Taking Your Time

Healing and rebuilding trust is not something that can be rushed. Trust takes time to rebuild, and it's essential to move at your own pace. The most important part of rebuilding trust is recognizing that it's okay to take small steps. Trusting someone again doesn't mean jumping back into a relationship with full emotional investment right away. Instead, it means allowing yourself the time and space to get comfortable with the idea of vulnerability again.

Setting Boundaries in Relationships

As you rebuild trust, it's important to establish clear boundaries. Boundaries allow you to protect yourself while still engaging with others. If someone makes you feel uncomfortable or crosses a line, it's important to assert your needs. Healthy relationships are built on mutual respect, and boundaries ensure that both parties feel safe and valued.

Seeking Supportive Relationships

When rebuilding relational trust, surround yourself with people who respect your boundaries, value your experiences, and offer unconditional support. These individuals are the ones who will help you heal, and their support will reinforce your belief in yourself and in healthy, trusting relationships.

Conclusion

Finding allies and support is an essential part of the healing journey after workplace bullying and gaslighting. Whether through shared stories in safe spaces, therapy, coaching, or peer support groups, community plays a vital role in helping you process your experience and reclaim your sense of self. Real support is not about fixing you, but about offering validation, empathy, and practical tools for healing. Rebuilding relational trust takes time, and it's important to move at your own pace, setting boundaries and seeking supportive relationships that nurture your growth. With the right community around you, healing becomes not only possible but also transformative, helping you step into a future filled with confidence, strength, and connection.

Chapter 11

Career Reclamation – Starting Fresh Without Carrying the Pain

Introduction

One of the most difficult aspects of recovering from workplace bullying and gaslighting is navigating the intersection of your emotional healing and your career. For many, the workplace is not just a place where we earn a living—it is an essential part of our identity, sense of purpose, and personal worth. When that environment becomes toxic, it doesn't just affect your professional life; it erodes your confidence, your mental health, and your sense of who you are.

As you work to heal from the wounds of workplace bullying, one question often arises: Should I stay, or should I go? This decision is not easy. It requires you to balance your emotional recovery with your professional goals. The thought of leaving may come with feelings of guilt, fear, or doubt. Yet, staying in a toxic environment can often prolong the pain, making recovery more difficult.

This chapter will help you navigate the challenging process of career reclamation—rebuilding your career and sense of self without carrying the emotional pain of past experiences. We'll explore the important questions to ask yourself when considering whether to stay or leave, how to navigate references, resumes, and trauma narratives, and how to rebrand your career identity so that you can thrive in a new professional environment. Finally, we will explore how to shift from merely surviving in your career to thriving in a fresh, healthy environment.

Is It Time to Stay or Go? Questions to Ask

Deciding whether to stay in your current job or leave is one of the most difficult decisions you will make after experiencing workplace bullying or gaslighting. On one hand, you may feel deeply connected to your work, the mission of the organization, or your colleagues. On the other hand, the emotional toll of being bullied or manipulated may have left you physically and mentally exhausted, making the idea of staying seem unbearable.

To help you decide whether it's time to stay or go, ask yourself the following questions:

1. How is my mental and physical health?

The most important question you need to ask yourself is about your overall well-being. Have you been experiencing chronic stress, burnout, anxiety, or physical symptoms like fatigue, sleep disturbances, or illness? If you are struggling with your mental or physical health, staying in a toxic environment may only exacerbate the damage. Your health should always be your top priority, and if staying in your current job is causing severe harm, it may be time to consider moving on.

2. Can I set boundaries here, or am I constantly being manipulated?

A healthy work environment allows you to set boundaries that protect your emotional and physical well-being. If you find that your boundaries are consistently ignored or violated, and if the emotional manipulation continues without support from management or HR, it may be a sign that the environment is not conducive to healing. If you can't establish boundaries or feel constantly undermined, leaving may be the best option.

3. Is there room for growth or recovery here?

Another important consideration is whether there is room for growth, both personally and professionally, in your current workplace. Are there opportunities to regain your confidence and rebuild your sense of self-worth? Is the organizational culture one that values respect, diversity, and healthy collaboration, or is it one where bullying and gaslighting are tolerated or ignored? If the workplace environment is unlikely to change or improve, and you do not see opportunities for personal growth, it may be worth considering a fresh start elsewhere.

4. How would I feel about leaving?

Think about how you would feel if you decided to leave. Would it provide relief and a sense of freedom, or would it be a decision filled with regret and guilt? Many survivors of workplace bullying feel guilty for leaving, especially if they have invested years in the organization or feel emotionally attached to the work. However, remember that leaving is not an admission of failure—it is an act of self-care and self-respect. If leaving brings you peace and clarity, it may be the right decision.

5. Can I find another job that aligns with my values and goals?

The fear of the unknown often prevents people from leaving toxic work environments. You may worry that there are no other opportunities out there or that you will not find a better fit. However, this fear can keep you stuck in a cycle of harm. Consider whether you can find a job that aligns more closely with your values, skills, and personal goals. Taking the leap may seem intimidating, but it can also open up new opportunities for personal and professional growth.

Navigating References, Resumes, and Trauma Narratives

Once you've made the decision to leave, the next step is to navigate the practical aspects of transitioning to a new job. For many survivors of workplace bullying, the idea of updating their resume, securing references, and explaining their experience to future employers can be fraught with anxiety. How do you explain a toxic work environment without damaging your career prospects? How do you address the emotional scars left behind by gaslighting while also presenting yourself as a strong and capable candidate?

Here's how to navigate this process:

1. Resume and References: Focus on Your Strengths

When updating your resume, it's important to focus on your achievements and strengths rather than the negative experiences that led you to leave. Highlight the skills you gained, the contributions you made, and the value you brought to your previous workplace. If you have worked in a toxic environment, it's still important to recognize the resilience and skills you developed as a result of that experience.

In terms of references, choose individuals who can speak to your professional abilities, character, and work ethic—ideally people who witnessed your contributions firsthand and who can offer a positive perspective on your work. If possible, avoid using individuals who were involved in the toxic dynamics of your past workplace, as this may unintentionally open old wounds or create unnecessary complications.

2. Trauma Narratives: Crafting Your Story

While it's important to remain positive on your resume and references, you also need to be prepared for the reality of explaining your departure during interviews. It's likely that you'll be asked about your reasons for leaving your previous role, and you should have a thoughtful, honest answer ready.

Here's how to craft your trauma narrative:

- **Keep it professional**: It's important to remain calm, professional, and focused on your growth and resilience rather than dwelling on the negativity of your past workplace. For example, you might say, "I left my previous position to seek a more supportive and collaborative work environment that aligns with my values."

- **Emphasize your learning and growth**: Frame your experience as an opportunity for growth. For instance, "While my previous role was challenging, I learned valuable lessons about resilience, setting boundaries, and advocating for myself. I'm now looking for a workplace that supports professional development and fosters mutual respect."

- **Don't overshare**: Avoid going into specific details about the bullying or gaslighting you experienced unless you feel it is absolutely necessary. If you do feel compelled to share, make sure that your response focuses on the lessons learned and the positive changes you are now seeking.

3. Seeking Professional Guidance

If you find the process of navigating references, resumes, and trauma narratives overwhelming, consider working with a career coach or therapist. A career coach can help you craft a compelling resume, guide you through the interview process, and build your confidence as you transition to a new role. A therapist can help you work through the emotional challenges of addressing your past while also offering guidance on how to heal and rebuild your career identity.

Rebranding Your Career Identity

Rebuilding your career after experiencing workplace bullying requires more than just updating your resume—it requires rebranding your professional identity. Many survivors of bullying internalize the negative messages they received, believing that they are not capable or deserving of success. Rebuilding your career identity is about shedding these false beliefs and reasserting who you are as a professional.

Here's how to begin the process of rebranding:

1. **Reconnect with Your Strengths**: Reflect on your achievements, skills, and experiences that you are proud of. What strengths did you develop over the course of your career? What unique qualities do you bring to the table? Reclaim your confidence by acknowledging these strengths and incorporating them into your new professional identity.

2. **Define Your Values**: Consider what values are most important to you in your career. What kind of work environment do you want to be a part of? What type of leadership style do you thrive under? When you are clear on your values, you can make intentional choices about the types of roles and organizations you want to work with.

3. **Create a New Narrative**: The way you talk about your career matters. Create a new narrative that frames your career as one of growth, resilience, and success. This new narrative is not about erasing your past but about emphasizing your ability to overcome challenges and emerge stronger.

4. **Set New Goals**: Rebuilding your career identity involves setting new professional goals that align with your values and aspirations. These goals should reflect your personal growth, your desire for a healthy work environment, and your ambitions for the future.

From Surviving to Thriving in a New Environment

Once you've rebuilt your career identity and reclaimed your confidence, it's time to shift from surviving to thriving in your new environment. Starting fresh can be daunting, but it also provides the opportunity to find a workplace that values you, respects your boundaries, and supports your growth.

To thrive in your new career environment, remember the following:

1. **Embrace Your Resilience**: You've already overcome significant challenges. Use that resilience to propel you forward in your new job, knowing that you can handle whatever comes your way.

2. **Seek Out Supportive Environments**: Choose workplaces that prioritize respect, collaboration, and personal well-being. Trust your instincts when evaluating potential employers and look for organizations that align with your values.

3. **Continue Your Healing Journey**: Healing from workplace bullying is ongoing. Continue to prioritize your mental health, practice self-care, and seek out support when needed. Allow yourself to grow, both professionally and personally, without carrying the pain of the past.

Conclusion

Career reclamation after workplace bullying is a powerful process of healing, growth, and transformation. Whether you choose to stay in your current job or move on to new opportunities, the key is to make decisions based on what is best for your mental health, well-being, and professional goals. Rebranding your career identity and shifting from survival to thriving is a gradual process, but with the right support, clarity, and focus, you can build a career that reflects your true value and potential. The pain you've endured does not define you—it is part of your story, but it is not your future. Reclaim your career, rebuild your confidence, and step into a brighter, healthier professional life.

Chapter 12

From Silent to Sovereign – Owning Your Narrative

Introduction

The journey of healing from workplace bullying and gaslighting involves not just reclaiming your emotional and physical well-being but also rewriting the story of your life. For many survivors, the experience of emotional abuse leaves a lasting mark on their identity, often becoming the central narrative of their lives. It's easy to define ourselves by the pain we've endured, letting the trauma shape how we see the world and ourselves. But true healing comes when we shift the narrative—from one of victimhood to one of sovereignty, empowerment, and personal growth.

In this chapter, we'll explore how to write a new story that is not centered around the abuse but rather on your strength, resilience, and the lessons you've learned. We'll look at how to transform pain into purpose, without falling into the trap of toxic positivity. We'll also explore how trauma can lead to deep personal growth, developing leadership skills, and fostering empathy for others. Finally, we'll discuss the power of mentoring, and when and how to help others who have been through the same painful experience. Owning your narrative is about reclaiming your story, stepping into your power, and using your experience to create a life that is meaningful and full of purpose.

Writing a New Story That's Not Centered on the Abuse

For many survivors of workplace bullying, the pain of the experience becomes a dominant part of their identity. It's understandable: after enduring gaslighting, manipulation, and emotional harm, it can feel like your life has been defined by the trauma. But while the abuse you experienced is undoubtedly a part of your story, it does not have to be the entire narrative. Rewriting your story is about shifting the focus from the pain and victimhood to empowerment, recovery, and future possibilities.

Changing the Focus of Your Story

To begin writing a new story, it's important to first acknowledge the pain you've experienced without letting it define who you are. Recognize that your past is part of you, but it doesn't dictate your future. The trauma you endured doesn't erase your strengths, your dreams, or your capacity for happiness. You are not just a survivor of bullying or gaslighting—you are a person of strength, resilience, and growth.

Here are some ways to rewrite your narrative:

1. **Acknowledge the Abuse Without Letting It Define You**: Begin by acknowledging that the bullying and gaslighting occurred, but don't allow those experiences to be the sole focus of your story. Yes, they were significant, but they are not the only

defining aspect of who you are. Recognize that while the past shaped you, it does not have to control you.

2. **Reclaim Your Power**: Moving from a victim mindset to a sovereign one is about reclaiming your power. Reflect on how far you've come in your healing journey—what have you learned? How have you grown? This is where you begin to shift the narrative from pain to empowerment.

3. **Identify Your Strengths**: Focus on the strengths and qualities that you discovered in yourself during your recovery. Perhaps you developed resilience, self-awareness, or an understanding of your emotional needs. Acknowledge these strengths and weave them into your new narrative. These are the parts of you that are truly enduring.

4. **Set New Goals and Intentions**: Start focusing on where you want to go, not where you've been. Write your future story— what goals do you want to achieve? What type of work environment do you want to cultivate for yourself? What kind of relationships do you want to build? Writing a new story involves focusing on what you want to create, not just what you've survived.

Transforming Pain into Purpose—Not Toxic Positivity

As you rewrite your narrative, one of the most important aspects is how you transform your pain into purpose. It's natural to want to make sense of what you've been through, but there is a risk of falling into the trap of toxic positivity—forcing yourself to view the trauma through a lens of "everything happens for a reason" or "it could have been worse." While it's important to find meaning in our struggles, it's equally important to honor our pain without glossing over it.

Pain as a Catalyst for Growth

Transforming pain into purpose is not about minimizing the hurt you've experienced or pretending that everything is fine. It's about finding meaning in your suffering and using that meaning to propel you forward. The key is to process your pain fully, allowing yourself to grieve and heal, before you begin the work of turning that pain into something positive.

Here's how to do this:

1. **Allow Yourself to Grieve**: Healing doesn't mean skipping over the pain—it means feeling it and giving yourself the space to mourn what you've lost. Grief is a natural part of healing, and it's necessary to fully process the trauma before you can move on to transformation.

2. **Use Your Experience to Help Others**: One powerful way to transform pain into purpose is by using your experience to help others who are going through similar struggles. Whether it's through mentorship, writing, or simply being a listening ear, using your pain as a source of empathy and support for others gives it meaning and purpose.

3. **Create New Opportunities for Yourself**: Pain often creates clarity. Once you have processed your grief, you can begin to use your pain as fuel to create new opportunities for yourself. Perhaps your experience has inspired you to pursue a new career path, start a new project, or get involved in a cause that matters to you. Transforming pain into purpose means taking action, not just finding meaning.

4. **Avoid Toxic Positivity**: Toxic positivity is the belief that we should always look for the silver lining in every situation, even when it feels inappropriate. It dismisses the reality of suffering and minimizes the emotional toll that trauma takes. While it's important to find hope and purpose, it's equally important to validate your feelings, acknowledge your pain, and not rush into finding "the lesson" before you're ready.

Personal Growth, Leadership, and Empathy After Trauma

One of the most beautiful outcomes of healing from workplace bullying is the personal growth that follows. Trauma doesn't just break us; it can also deepen us. If you approach the healing process with intention and patience, it can lead to profound changes in your character, leadership abilities, and capacity for empathy. You can emerge from your struggles not just as a survivor but as someone who is stronger, wiser, and more compassionate.

Personal Growth

Trauma often forces us to confront parts of ourselves we've neglected or ignored. It makes us question our values, our boundaries, and our needs. In this process of self-reflection, we grow. The person you become after healing is likely to be more self-aware, more resilient, and more committed to creating a life that aligns with your true desires. Personal growth after trauma often involves:

- **Reassessing Your Priorities**: After experiencing bullying, many people begin to reassess what truly matters to them. You might find that your career, relationships, or lifestyle no longer align with your values. Personal growth is about making the changes necessary to live a life that reflects who you truly are.

- **Developing Emotional Intelligence**: Going through trauma often leads to an increased understanding of emotions—both your own and others'. This is a vital component of personal growth, as it helps you navigate relationships and make more informed decisions in the future.

- **Building Self-Confidence**: As you heal and reclaim your sense of self-worth, you develop greater confidence in your abilities, your decisions, and your intuition. This newfound confidence becomes an important part of your identity moving forward.

Leadership and Empathy

Healing from trauma can also make you a more effective leader. Having experienced emotional hardship, you may find that you have a greater capacity for empathy, understanding, and support for others. People who have been through trauma often excel in leadership roles because they are more attuned to the needs of others and more willing to foster an environment of respect and safety.

As a leader, you may choose to:

- **Lead with Empathy**: Use your experience to cultivate a leadership style that values emotional intelligence and compassion. Recognize the importance of creating a supportive and respectful environment for your colleagues or team.

- **Encourage Vulnerability**: Encourage others to be open about their challenges and emotional needs. Leading by example and fostering an environment where vulnerability is seen as a strength rather than a weakness can help prevent future toxic environments.

- **Support Growth in Others**: As you heal, you may feel compelled to mentor or support others who are going through similar struggles. Whether it's through formal mentoring or informal conversations, helping others navigate their own journey is a powerful way to give back and foster a supportive community.

When and How to Mentor Others Who've Been Through the Same

Mentoring others who have experienced the same trauma can be one of the most fulfilling aspects of your healing journey. It allows you to share your wisdom, offer support, and help others navigate the difficult path toward recovery. However, it's important to recognize that mentoring is not about "fixing" others—it's about walking alongside them, offering guidance, and creating a safe space for them to heal.

When to Mentor

You should begin mentoring others when you feel emotionally ready and have made significant progress in your own healing journey. Mentorship should come from a place of strength, not from a place of unresolved pain. Once you have developed a deeper understanding of your own experiences and how to heal from them, you'll be in a better position to offer guidance to others.

How to Mentor

- **Listen First**: Before offering advice, listen to the other person's story. Understanding their experience will help you offer more empathetic and personalized support.

- **Share Your Story, But Don't Lead with It**: Your story can serve as a powerful tool for inspiration, but it's important to also allow the person you are mentoring to share their experiences without feeling overshadowed by yours.

- **Set Boundaries**: As a mentor, it's important to recognize your own limits. You are not responsible for "fixing" someone else's trauma, and it's essential to take care of your own emotional well-being while offering support.

- **Encourage Empowerment**: Instead of simply offering solutions, encourage the person you are mentoring to find their own path to healing. Support them in finding their voice, trusting their instincts, and making decisions that are in their best interest.

Conclusion

Reclaiming your narrative after workplace bullying and gaslighting is one of the most empowering steps you can take in your healing journey. By writing a new story that is not centered on the abuse, transforming pain into purpose, and using your experience to foster personal growth, leadership, and empathy, you can move from surviving to thriving. Owning your narrative allows you to step into your power, embrace your full potential, and create a life filled with meaning, resilience, and authenticity. When you are ready, mentoring others who have been through similar experiences is a natural extension of your healing—a way to give back, support others, and build a community of strength.

Chapter 13

Living Unapologetically – Freedom, Peace, and Emotional Safety

Introduction

The journey from surviving workplace bullying and gaslighting to living unapologetically is not linear, but it is powerful. For so long, you may have lived in a world where fear, doubt, and self-censorship ruled your interactions. The trauma from bullying and emotional manipulation likely forced you to question yourself, your worth, and your ability to trust. But as you heal, the goal is to reclaim your life and live it fully—without apology, fear, or the weight of past experiences holding you back. This is the journey toward freedom, peace, and emotional safety—where you are no longer defined by the wounds of the past but by the strength and healing you have achieved.

In this chapter, we'll explore how to live a life that doesn't revolve around fear, how to choose workplaces and relationships that honor your value, and why emotional safety must be non-negotiable. We will also reflect on the ultimate truth that, though you may have endured hardship, you are not your wounds—you are your healing. Living unapologetically means embracing your truth, asserting your worth, and choosing a future where you thrive, not just survive.

Living a Life That Doesn't Revolve Around Fear

For too long, workplace bullying and gaslighting can keep you trapped in a cycle of fear. Fear of being criticized, rejected, or invalidated. Fear of conflict or standing up for yourself. Fear of being "too much" or "too sensitive." These fears become internalized, limiting your ability to fully live and engage with the world around you. Living unapologetically begins with breaking free from these fears and reclaiming the freedom to be yourself, without hesitation.

Breaking Free from Fear

The first step in living unapologetically is to acknowledge the fears that were planted in you during your time in a toxic environment. It's important to recognize that these fears were often not yours to begin with; they were the result of manipulation and emotional harm. They don't define you—they are remnants of the past that have no place in your future.

To move beyond fear, consider these strategies:

1. **Identify the Source of Your Fear**: Take time to reflect on the fears that still affect you. Are they related to specific situations, people, or emotions from your past workplace? Once you identify where the fear is coming from, you can begin to deconstruct it. Understand that these fears may have been necessary for survival in a toxic environment, but they are no longer serving you.

2. **Challenge Your Fear**: Fear often holds power because it remains unchallenged. Start by questioning the validity of your fears. Ask yourself, "What's the worst that could happen if I speak my truth?" Often, the fear we feel is far worse than the reality. Challenge your fear by taking small steps—whether it's asserting yourself in a conversation or voicing your opinion in a meeting. Every time you act despite fear, you diminish its control over you.

3. **Practice Courage Over Comfort**: Living unapologetically means choosing courage over comfort. It's easier to stay silent, to conform, or to appease others, but true freedom comes when you choose to speak up, take risks, and live authentically—even when it feels uncomfortable. You don't need to be fearless, but you can practice acting in spite of fear.

4. **Surround Yourself with Support**: When you're surrounded by supportive, validating people, the fears that once ruled you begin to lose their grip. Surround yourself with individuals who encourage you to speak your truth, set boundaries, and live authentically. These positive influences will help you overcome fear and step into your power.

Living With Freedom and Peace

Living without fear isn't just about eliminating negative emotions—it's about actively choosing peace and freedom in every aspect of your life. This means reclaiming your emotional autonomy, honoring your needs, and asserting your worth, regardless of external opinions.

Living a life centered on freedom and peace means:

- **Creating Emotional Space**: Free yourself from the toxic influences of your past. Whether it's quitting a job that doesn't honor you or distancing yourself from people who bring negativity into your life, clearing emotional space is a crucial part of living unapologetically.

- **Cultivating Inner Calm**: Practices like meditation, journaling, or mindfulness can help you cultivate inner peace. These practices allow you to connect with yourself and experience life without the constant anxiety or fear that once dictated your responses.

- **Enjoying Authenticity**: When you live authentically, you are no longer hiding parts of yourself to please others or avoid conflict. You can express your true thoughts, needs, and desires without fear of judgment or rejection.

Choosing Workplaces and People That Honor Your Value

As you move forward in your career and relationships, it is essential to choose environments and people that align with your values, needs, and emotional well-being. After surviving a toxic workplace, you deserve to be in spaces where respect, trust, and empathy are the norms—not the exception.

Choosing Healthy Work Environments

The process of career reclamation goes beyond finding a job—it's about finding a workplace that values you, your well-being, and your contributions. Here's how to identify work environments that support your healing and growth:

1. **Prioritize Emotional Safety**: Emotional safety must be a non-negotiable for any workplace you choose. Look for companies or organizations that have a track record of promoting mental health, providing clear avenues for reporting misconduct, and respecting work-life balance. Avoid workplaces that dismiss employee well-being or tolerate toxic behavior.

2. **Look for Alignment with Your Values**: Choose a job where the organization's mission and values align with your own. When you believe in the work you do and the company culture, you will feel a greater sense of purpose and fulfillment. Seek out workplaces that value collaboration, integrity, and respect—values that align with your own.

3. **Trust Your Instincts**: After experiencing bullying, your instincts about workplace dynamics and relationships will become sharper. Trust your gut when evaluating new job opportunities. If something feels off or the work environment seems toxic, listen to that inner voice and consider it a red flag.

4. **Set Boundaries from the Start**: In your new role, be proactive about setting clear boundaries. From the very beginning, make sure that your new workplace understands that respect and

emotional safety are non-negotiable. These boundaries will help you establish a healthy, professional relationship with your colleagues and prevent toxic behavior from taking root.

Choosing Healthy Relationships

The people you surround yourself with—both in your personal life and in the workplace—play a vital role in your healing and growth. You deserve relationships that are reciprocal, supportive, and grounded in mutual respect. Here's how to choose people who honor your value:

1. **Seek Out Empathetic, Respectful Individuals**: Look for people who listen to you, validate your feelings, and provide emotional support when needed. These individuals will help you feel seen, heard, and valued, which is essential for healing after trauma.

2. **Learn to Recognize Healthy Dynamics**: Healthy relationships are built on trust, communication, and mutual respect. If someone constantly undermines you, manipulates you, or makes you feel less than, they are not honoring your value. Recognize these behaviors early on and protect yourself from toxic relationships.

3. **Give Yourself Permission to Walk Away**: It's okay to walk away from relationships that are draining, abusive, or toxic. You don't owe anyone your time or energy if they are not treating you with respect and empathy. Let go of relationships that hinder

your growth and make space for those who uplift and support you.

Emotional Safety as a Non-Negotiable

After experiencing gaslighting and workplace bullying, emotional safety becomes a non-negotiable. Emotional safety is the foundation upon which all healthy relationships—whether personal or professional—are built. It means creating a space where your emotions, boundaries, and identity are respected without fear of manipulation, criticism, or harm.

What Emotional Safety Looks Like

Emotional safety is characterized by:

- **Respect for Boundaries**: Others respect your personal space, time, and emotional needs without pushing you to compromise them.

- **Validation**: Your feelings, thoughts, and experiences are acknowledged and accepted, even if others don't always agree with you.

- **Support, Not Control**: Healthy relationships are based on mutual support, not control or manipulation. Emotional safety involves giving and receiving support without the fear of being coerced or invalidated.

- **Open Communication**: People in emotionally safe environments communicate openly, honestly, and respectfully. There's no fear of judgment or reprisal for speaking your truth.

Creating emotional safety as a non-negotiable means setting firm boundaries, advocating for yourself, and only allowing those who respect you to enter your life.

Epilogue

The truth that you are not your wounds, but rather your healing, is one of the most important lessons you can take with you as you move forward in your life. The trauma of workplace bullying and gaslighting may have shaped your past, but it does not define your future. Healing is a continual process, and it requires patience, self-compassion, and commitment.

As you live unapologetically, you create a life centered around freedom, peace, and emotional safety. You make choices that honor your worth and bring you closer to your authentic self. You learn to trust yourself again and set boundaries that protect your emotional well-being. You embrace the lessons of your past without letting them dictate your future. And you recognize that, while your wounds are part of your story, they are not who you are.

Your healing is the most powerful part of your narrative. It is the testament to your resilience, your strength, and your ability to thrive despite adversity. When you live unapologetically, you reclaim your life and step into a future filled with purpose, peace, and the unwavering knowledge that you are worthy of all the joy, success, and love life has to offer.

You are not defined by your pain. You are defined by your healing, your growth, and your unwavering commitment to living a life that honors your truth.

The journey from the invisible scars of workplace bullying and gaslighting to the freedom of reclaiming your confidence, voice, and emotional safety is a transformative one. Throughout this book, we have explored the emotional, psychological, and professional toll that bullying and gaslighting can have on individuals. From understanding the complex dynamics of workplace abuse to navigating the aftermath and rebuilding a life that honors your value, this process is about rediscovering who you are, regaining your power, and living unapologetically.

We began by learning what workplace bullying really looks like and how gaslighting undermines our perception of reality, making it difficult to even recognize the abuse when it's happening. But understanding these behaviors is the first step toward reclaiming your truth. We also validated the emotional impact of bullying, making it clear that the myth of being "too sensitive" only serves to silence survivors and corrode their mental health. We explored why bullies target certain individuals—not because of weakness, but because of strength—and how leadership dynamics and groupthink often perpetuate the silence that allows abuse to thrive.

We looked into the "snap" moment when you realize the abuse isn't your fault, and the aftermath—burnout, anxiety, and the emotional, physical, and career damage that persists long after the abuse ends. We empowered you with the language to name your experiences, to break the silence without breaking yourself, and to reclaim your narrative.

We discussed the essential process of rebuilding emotional boundaries and recognizing the difference between fear-driven walls and healthy limits. We focused on the reclamation of your confidence—how to rebuild self-trust, quiet the inner critic, and embrace your steady, unwavering sense of worth. We guided you through an emotional detox—releasing the residue of gaslighting and reprogramming your internalized doubts with affirmations, journal prompts, and grounding practices.

We emphasized the importance of community and how shared stories and safe spaces can provide the healing support you need. We introduced the concept of career reclamation, giving you tools to navigate new professional opportunities without carrying the weight of past trauma. We explored how to write a new story for yourself—one that isn't centered around the abuse but instead focused on growth, leadership, and empathy for others who have experienced similar struggles.

Finally, we learned that living unapologetically is not just about freedom from the past—it's about creating a life grounded in emotional safety, peace, and the pursuit of work and relationships that honor your value. The ultimate reflection from this journey is that **you are not your wounds**; you are your healing. This journey is not one of perfection, but of continual growth, reclamation, and the courage to live freely and authentically.

As you move forward, remember that recovery is not a destination, but a continuous process. The scars of the past do not define you—they are a testament to your resilience, strength, and capacity for healing. You have reclaimed your voice, your confidence, and your peace. Now, you can live unapologetically, grounded in the truth of who you are and the beauty of your journey toward freedom.

www.ingramcontent.com/pod-product-compliance
Lightning Source LLC
Chambersburg PA
CBHW071518120626
46550CB00006B/2269